Managing Business Risk

TENTH EDITION

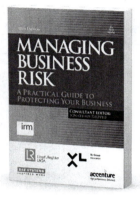

Managing Business Risk

A practical guide to protecting your business

Consultant editor:
Jonathan Reuvid

KoganPage

LONDON PHILADELPHIA NEW DELHI

First published in Great Britain and the United States in 2003 by Kogan Page Limited
Second edition 2005
Third edition 2006
Fourth edition 2007
Fifth edition 2008
Sixth edition 2009
Seventh edition 2010
Eighth edition 2012
Ninth edition 2013
Tenth edition 2014

2nd Floor, 45 Gee Street
London EC1V 3RS
United Kingdom
www.koganpage.com

1518 Walnut Street, Suite 1100
Philadelphia PA 19102
USA

4737/23 Ansari Road
Daryaganj
New Delhi 110002
India

ISBN   978 0 7494 7043 2
E-ISBN   978 0 7494 7044 9

British Library Cataloguing-in-Publication Data

A CIP record for this book is available from the British Library.

Library of Congress Cataloging-in-Publication Data

Managing business risk : a practical guide to protecting your business / [edited by] Jonathan Reuvid. – Tenth edition.
    pages cm
    ISBN 978-0-7494-7043-2 (hardback) – ISBN 978-0-7494-7044-9 (ebook)   1. Risk management.
I. Reuvid, Jonathan.
    HD61.M26 2014
    658.15'5–dc23
                                                                                               2014015340

Typeset by Graphicraft Limited, Hong Kong
Printed and bound by CPI Group (UK) Ltd, Croydon CR0 4YY

CONTENTS

FOREWORD

All business has always involved risk – indeed, it is in the very essence of enterprise to do so. In recent years though, things seem to have reached a whole new level. Never has risk been so unrelenting, immediate, diverse or potentially devastating – or at least, that's the perception painted by many of our media.

Too many businesses, though, continue to focus on the negative risks that are in the news this month. Instead of this approach – so-called 'risk management by media' – they should be guided by their own strategic objectives.

This sort of effective risk management offers true strategic advantage. It must never become a technical discipline peddled by technocrats whom nobody understands. Instead, it has to be a strategic and people-focused discipline, with strong elements of financial and statistical competence, coupled with a good grasp of history, futurology and common sense all thrown in for good measure.

Today's world is indeed infinitely more complex and interconnected than that of our parents or grandparents. We are truly living through so-called VUCA – volatile, uncertain, complex and ambiguous – times.

Whilst simple risks are comparatively easy to identify, quantify and understand, there are three areas in particular that I'd suggest companies should devote more attention to.

Firstly, high-impact, low-frequency events. These are the so-called 'black swans': those things you'd never think of, nor expect, to happen. Yet paradigm shift is very real and remarkably commonplace: think of how MP3 files have replaced LPs, cassettes and CDs, or how hybrid vehicle drives now threaten established internal combustion technologies in the same way that these replaced steam and horse power. There is no substitute here to stretching the imagination, networking far and wide, and thinking the unthinkable.

Secondly, interconnections between risks. Most firms will consider their suppliers' risks but how many really devote time to looking at their customers' risks, or indeed the risks posed by their suppliers' suppliers? The 'extended enterprise' has come of age, and businesses must adjust their risk management strategies accordingly. At a global level, interconnectivity between economies is increasingly recognized to be not just a driver for global growth but also a major systemic factor in the risk of potential global fiscal meltdown.

Finally, culture, compensation and fraud continue to be major drivers of value loss in firms. How many of us wake up each day to ask 'who's next?' when it comes to corporate corruption?

This book provides invaluable guidance in some of today's most important areas for businesses to keep sight of: boardroom governance, information security, operational risks and emerging market threats. Boards today need to keep sight of all these areas, as well as the ultimate risks posed by market and product competition.

Competence in risk management is paramount to business survival and success.

Steve Fowler, Strategic Advisor to the Board, the Institute of Risk Management, and
Principal, Amarreurs Consulting

CONTRIBUTORS' NOTES

Ben Allgrove is a partner in Baker & McKenzie's London office, whose practice includes a mix of contentious and non-contentious work in the technology space. His practice includes acting on major IP and IT disputes, as well as advising on e-commerce, data protection, content licensing and other IP issues, regulation, freedom of information and transactional work. Ben also has considerable lobbying experience, especially on copyright and broadcast regulation. He has been recognized as a leading technology lawyer, described in Chambers by clients as 'phenomenal' and having 'a very deep understanding' of technology issues.

Gerard Bloom is Chief Underwriting Officer for Financial Institutions at XL Group. He has 20 years' experience in the London and international markets. Joining XL Group in 2009, Gerard has contributed to the considerable growth of the FI portfolio and today XL Group is one of the largest insurers of financial institutions globally. Previously, Gerard worked at Zurich Insurance, AIG and Willis Group. He is based at XL Group's London office but spends much of his time travelling to clients and brokers around the world. He has spoken extensively at seminars and events on related topics for financial institutions, including crime exposures, directors' liabilities and operational risk.

James Borshell is a senior associate in the UK Pensions team at Dentons UKMEA LLP where he advises clients on a mix of scheme and corporate related issues. He has over 10 years' experience advising on UK pensions matters including a 5-year stint spent in the civil service drafting legislation following the introduction of the Pensions Act 2004 regulatory regime.

Ben Cattaneo is a manager at Accenture Risk Management and works within Accenture's Cross-Industry and Resources team. Based in London, Ben possesses over 12 years' experience helping clients assess, quantify and manage political risk, design and implement enterprise risk management (ERM) programmes and manage acute crises. He combines deep risk management expertise with strategy and change management skills to help clients become and remain high-performing businesses.

Steve Culp is Senior Managing Director, Accenture Finance & Risk Services. Based in London, he has more than 20 years of global experience in strategy definition, risk management, enterprise performance management and delivering large-scale finance operations engagements. Prior to his current role, Steve was the global lead for Accenture's Finance & Performance Management consulting services for global banking, insurance and capital markets institutions. With his extensive risk management and performance management experience and business acumen, Steve guides executives and their teams on the journey to becoming high-performance businesses.

Carlo Gallo has helped dozens of multinationals make crucial investment decisions. In 2013 Dr Gallo founded Enquirisk, an innovative online platform that helps organizations to efficiently access country, industry and risk expertise. From late 2005 until April 2012 he was Control Risks' lead political risk analyst on Russia/former Soviet Union states. With Control Risks, he has published hundreds of timely analytical briefs on business risk developments in Russia, Ukraine, Belarus and other countries of the region. Dr Gallo has also authored dozens of in-depth political risk reports looking into virtually all sectors of the Russian economy. Previously, he has completed a PhD in Russian politics at the LSE and has held lecturing and research positions at leading UK universities.

Allan Gifford is an experienced enterprise risk management (ERM) advisor, having designed, implemented and assessed enterprise-wide risk management frameworks for organizations globally. He is a certified ISO 31000 professional, an approved ISO 31000 lead trainer, and member of the Institute of Risk Management and Institute of Operational Risk.

Stephen Gill is an experienced international business manager and company director with a strong engineering background, much of whose experience was gained at senior management or board level. Stephen's active involvement in Asia began over a decade ago after being brought in to manage a failing joint-venture company in Shanghai and he has experienced at first hand the highs and lows of business in Asia and Asia Pacific. Currently based in Bangkok, he has recently managed the development of South-East Asia sales strategies for two multinational engineering groups. Stephen is a regular contributor to business and technical magazines and books, as well as a conference speaker. He has an MBA from Loughborough University and an LLM (Business Law) from De Montfort University. Stephen Gill Associates are a multi-award-winning consultancy, most recently winning a Stevie Award.

Cor Groenveld is the Global Head of Food Supply Chain Services at Lloyd's Register Quality Assurance (LRQA). He has a degree in food technology and spent 10 years in the food industry before joining LRQA. His background includes being a quality assurance manager, working in product development and production as well as logistics in the confectionery and convenience food industry. Before taking on his current role, Cor was an assessor manager, lead auditor, trainer and service developer at LRQA. Cor's other relevant activities include: Chairman of the Board of the Foundation for Food Safety (owner of the FSSC 22000 certification scheme); representative of the Independent International Organisation for Certification (IIOC) on the Food Safety Working Group of the European Accreditation Committee; and member of the ISO working group for food and food safety standards (ISO 22000), the food committee of the Dutch Normalisation Committee (NEN) and the technical committee of the Global Food Safety Initiative (GFSI).

Steve Holmes is a partner in the Information Technology & Communications practice at Baker & McKenzie's London office. Steve leads the sourcing team in London and is a member of the European IT/communications steering group. He spends the majority of his time negotiating major sourcing, technology and digital media contracts. Steve's recent experience in sourcing includes network, technology and business process out-sourcing deals, deals for the licensing and implementation of systems, and cloud-based deals for both customers and suppliers in a range of industries, including media, telecoms and professional services. He has been recognized for a number of years as a leading outsourcing, technology, telecoms and media lawyer in Chambers, which praises him 'for his technical expertise, in particular his drafting skills'. Steve is described by clients as 'thorough, tenacious and always keen to defend his clients' interests'.

Chris Jackson is a legal risk specialist and a partner with Burges Salmon's Dispute Resolution practice. He has a track record of success in large and complex commercial disputes and has achieved national recognition in rail and health and safety. He regularly works with businesses in a number of sectors advising on strategic risk and risk management. Chris also regularly provides training to directors and senior management of major organizations on legal risk and major incident response.

Sinead Kelly is an associate and professional support lawyer in the Corporate Department at A & L Goodbody. Based in the primary office in Dublin, Eire, Sinead's areas of expertise include corporate governance, compliance, directors' duties and responsibilities and company law. She also writes extensively on these and other areas of corporate law.

Theo Ling is a Baker & McKenzie partner and Chair of the firm's Global Privacy and Information Management Leadership Team. His international commercial/regulatory practice is focused on technology-based issues and the computer, internet and communications industries. Mr Ling is recognized for his creative, pragmatic and solution-based approach, which he applies when helping businesses develop and implement effective global strategies to support multi-jurisdictional commercial activities and manage complex cross-border compliance risks. Based in Toronto, he is lead editor of BakerGPS, a virtual privacy think-tank.

Neil Maclean is a partner and Head of Employment at Shepherd & Wedderburn, Edinburgh. Neil has strong experience of managing complex business transfers and restructuring programmes, involving TUPE and redundancy, collective consultation and industrial relations issues. He provides excellent corporate support with experience across a wide range of sectors. Neil is a strategic thinker and also keenly pragmatic and commercial. He is an experienced advocate in both the employment and employment appeals tribunals. Neil has also been successful in using mediation as a route to resolve disputes promptly and commercially. Chambers and Partners, which lists Neil as a leader in his field, remarks that he is 'extremely sharp and knowledgeable' as well as 'an excellent communicator'.

Doris Myles is a senior lawyer in the IT/commercial department of Baker & McKenzie in London. Her role as a professional support lawyer is to support the department by applying the legal skills and experience she gained as an associate to contribute towards know-how, legal updates, precedent and practice notes, training and business development. She holds an MSc in Management of Intellectual Property Law from the University of London and also a postgraduate Diploma in Intellectual Property Law from Bristol University.

Gavin O'Toole is an energetic professional with more than 23 years' experience in newspaper journalism as a writer and editor at the UK's most prominent newspapers. Among his editorial achievements have been spells as Commissioning Editor, Special Reports at the *Financial Times,* Revise Sub-editor at *The Observer* and Launch Production Editor of the *Education Guardian.* Gavin is also Founding Editorial Director of the Aflame literary publishing house and a member of the American Series advisory board, Texas Tech University Press. As a freelance journalist and copy-editor since September 2012 his clients include *International Financing Review*, *Guardian Online*, Al Jazeera and Kogan Page.

Gavin has doctoral-level expertise in Latin America with an academic teaching record and is fluent in Spanish. Having graduated from the University of Liverpool, he was awarded an MA with Distinction at the Institute of Latin American Studies, London, in 1995 and a PhD from Queen Mary, University of London in 2012.

James M Pearson is CEO of Pacific Risk Advisors Ltd and advises on the strategic and sustainability risk management needs of financial and real estate investors in Asia. He has over 20 years' experience in the international sustainability risk consultancy industry, and has been located in the United Kingdom, Hong Kong and Thailand. His extensive management consultancy experience includes project management and direction of multi-jurisdictional and multi-facility studies addressing business and management risks from an environmental, social, governance awareness and sustainable perspective.

Bennett G Picker is a senior counsel at the Philadelphia law firm of Stradley Ronon where he is a full-time mediator and arbitrator in complex business disputes. He is a distinguished fellow, International Academy of Mediators; member of the National Panel of Distinguished Neutrals, CPR Institute for Dispute Resolutions; and a certified mediator, International Mediator Institute. He received from the American Bar Association its annual 'Lawyer As Problem Solver' award. Mr Picker is the author of *Mediation Practice Guide: A handbook for resolving business disputes (second edition)*, published by the American Bar Association Dispute Resolution Section. He has written extensively and lectured widely in the United States and Europe on mediation, negotiations and arbitration and has served as a member of the Executive Committee of the American Arbitration Association.

Ron Reid heads the regulatory team at Shoosmiths LLP. He is based at their Milton Keynes office and specializes in business compliance and crisis management issues. He regularly advises and defends clients facing prosecution for corporate crime and breaches of health and safety, environmental, trading standards and other regulatory legislation. Ron has previously advised the Health & Safety Executive on complex matters. He has been identified as a leader in the area of health and safety, licensing and product liability (food) by Chambers and Partners for almost 20 years and by the Legal 500 in 2013 as having 'detailed practical knowledge of health and safety'. Ron also heads up Shoosmiths' Occupational Safety (SOS) team offering a comprehensive occupational safety service to clients including pre-emptive advice and full audits, risk assessment and training. In addition, he is the honorary legal adviser to the Inter-Company Consumer Affairs Association, a trade association of consumer managers in the food and drink manufacturing industry, and to the London Food Club. Ron regularly delivers papers to regional, national and international seminars as well as in-house and external management training courses which are designed and tailored to individual client needs, including e-learning courses to assist clients in fields such as Bribery Act compliance and personal safety. He is a director of the Radon Council.

Jonathan Reuvid has more than 25 years' experience of joint venture development and start-ups in China. An Oxford MA with a degree in Politics, Philosophy and Economics he worked first as an economist for the French national oil company, Total, before moving into financial services and consultancy. He joined a Fortune 500 US multinational in 1978, where he became Director of European Operations before engaging with China in the mid-1980s for clients and on his own behalf. In 1989 Jonathan started a third career as a writer and editor of business books for Kogan Page and has more than 80 editions of 35 titles to his name, including nine editions of *Managing Business Risk*, three editions of *The Handbook of International Trade*, five editions of *Doing Business with China*, two editions of *Business Insights: China*, and investment guides to each of the European states that became EU members in 2004 and, more recently, Morocco. He is a founder director of a conference management company, specializing in business areas such as advanced patent management strategies, data risk management in financial services and infrastructure investment and of a company offering an online platform for the exchange of copyright licenses.

Katie Russell is an experienced advisor in UK employment law at Shepherd & Wedderburn. She is dual qualified and has over six years' city experience. Katie advises on a broad range of matters, from ad hoc HR queries and redundancy exercises to pension scheme closures and high-value bonus claims. She also regularly advises on corporate reorganizations, outsourcings, acquisitions and disposals and has particular expertise in financial services.

Martin Sutherland is the Managing Director of BAE Systems Applied Intelligence, the Security Division of BAE Systems. He has held the position of Managing Director since 2008 when BAE Systems acquired the company (formerly Detica) and Martin led the post-acquisition integration into BAE Systems. Applied Intelligence is now a global security business, serving customers across the Americas, Europe and Asia Pacific with intelligence, counter fraud and cyber security solutions.

Martin's early career was with Andersen Consulting (now Accenture) and British Telecom (BT) in technical and business consulting roles. He joined Detica in 1996 focusing primarily on secure government programmes. He held a number of director roles within the business prior to becoming MD, notably setting up a commercial security group, launching Detica's counter fraud business and latterly running the Government business in the UK.

He is a member of the UKTI Security Sector Advisory Group and the joint industry government Cyber Growth Partnership. He is also a regular contributor to the press on issues relating to cyber security.

He holds an MA in Physics from Oxford University and a Master's of Science from Imperial and UCL, London University, and is a governor of his children's school.

Jonathan Tam is an articling student in the Toronto office of Baker & McKenzie LLP. He received his law degree from the University of Toronto and his undergraduate degree from Harvard University. He has assisted on numerous projects for multi-national companies with a focus on technology and international commerce.

Ian Tucker is a senior development lawyer with Burges Salmon's Dispute Resolution practice. He works across a range of sectors dealing with commercial disputes and regulatory and risk issues, including advising on rail industry disputes and corporate risk and liability. Ian regularly advises on new regulations including the implementation of European law, corporate structure and risk and regulatory enforcement. He also advises on risk management, compliance and investigation and the regulatory framework for safety.

Henrietta Watchorn is an associate in Squire Sanders' Employment team in London. Henrietta trained with the firm and completed a secondment at a major supermarket group where she worked alongside the HR and policy team. Her experience includes advising clients on a range of contentious and non-contentious employment matters including redundancy queries, performance management queries and dismissals, drafting and reviewing handbooks and various employment policies, advising and assisting clients with the defence of employment tribunal claims and advising on the terms of settlement agreements. Henrietta also provides in-house training on employment law to clients.

David Whincup is a partner and Head of Squire Sanders' London Employment practice. His expertise gained from nearly 30 years as a specialist employment law practitioner covers a variety of employment-related issues including recruitment, drafting, disciplinary and grievance procedures, redundancies, discrimination and dismissal claims and other litigation, whistleblowing, employee health, data protection and matters surrounding confidentiality and IP in the workplace. David is a well-known speaker on employment matters, both in-house to clients and for commercial training providers, and is a regular contributor to various employment publications. He is a CEDR-qualified mediator and has been a constant fixture in the Chambers and Legal 500 directories for over 10 years.

Introduction

As directors and senior managers focus on moving their businesses forward during the current recovery phase from recession, it would be easy to forget those concerns and risks which have come to the forefront during the prolonged period of austerity. However, the risk of fall-out remains from many of the issues which forced themselves on the attention of boardrooms and senior management over the past five years, as well as new risks which have emerged from recent regulatory changes and reforms and from which the full impact has yet to be felt. Therefore, we have chosen to devote the first three parts of this tenth edition of *Managing Business Risk* to a selection of these risk issues and their management.

Part One

In Part One five issues are selected of continuing concern to directors. The opening chapter from the first of our regular contributors, Accenture's Ben Cattaneo, offers professional advice on how to exploit business opportunity from resilience to volatility and uncertainty, hallmarks of everyone's recessionary experience.

Many corporates have learned from the bitter experience of lengthy business disputes that the cost in terms of money, management time and lost opportunities of litigation can be prohibitive, and will remain hesitant to pursue future well-founded claims in the courts. In the second chapter, Bennett Picker of Stradley Ronon Stevens & Young, a leading US mediation lawyer and the first of the two North American law firms writing for this edition, explains how business disputes can be managed and resolved more effectively and painlessly through professional mediation and negotiation.

The next chapter reviews the incidence and effects of corporate greed in today's capitalist environment. Gerard Bloom of XL Group, a longstanding contributor to the book, reflects on the desire to make money as a driver of capitalism and the role of insurance as a risk mitigant, placing the onus on financial institutions to get corporate culture right by empowering risk managers to manage the framework within which they control unacceptable risks. There are no panaceas and the issue of corporate greed will doubtless run and run.

There are significant changes in train from the regulatory reform of UK employment law to which readers are alerted in the fourth chapter by Neil Maclean and Katie Russell of Shepherd & Wedderburn. The final chapter of Part One by Chris Jackson and Ian Tucker of Burges Salmon addresses another perennial topic of boardroom frustration: contracts that turn out not to reflect the agreements that signatories thought they had reached. Having examined the risks posed, the authors suggest potential solutions.

Part Two

Part Two is devoted to information and online risks and opens with an authoritative chapter from Martin Sutherland, BAE Systems Detica, another regular contributor to the book and a global leader in the management of cyber-security, in which he provides a lucid explanation of the nature of cyber-security risk and suggests approaches at boardroom level to balancing risk governance and proactive opportunity management.

Theo Ling and Jonathan Tam of Baker & McKenzie, the second of the North American law firms contributing to this edition, define responsibilities for information accountability and best governance practices for its achievement within the context of the Global Privacy Enforcement Network.

In the context of EU regulation, Doris Myles, Ben Allgrove and Steve Holmes of Baker & McKenzie's UK practice review the requirements of the EU Consumer Rights Directive and its effects as it is enacted. In the narrower field of the UK financial sector, I have provided a commentary on the Bank of England's 2013 Systemic Risk Survey which is relevant to the banking sectors of all advanced economies.

Part Three

The range of Part Three extends from topics of operational risk authored by four regular contributors to key employment issues by three new *Managing Business Risk* authors. Food safety, particularly in respect of products sold through supermarket chains, has become a headline topic in the UK over the past year and the necessary risk management disciplines are addressed in the first chapter by Cor Groenveld of Lloyd's Register Quality Assurance.

The over-arching role of risk management in achieving enhanced performance is examined next by Alan Gifford, the specialist consultant in another of his thought-provoking chapters. For the third chapter on achieving improved standards of risk management in the supply chain, we have reprised an Accenture chapter from the last edition which remains wholly pertinent, and in the fourth chapter Ron Reid writes on the continuing need to manage health and safety and environmental risk effectively.

Moving on to employment issues, Sinead Kelly of A & L Goodbody discusses the UK Corporate Governance Code requirements for women on boards in the context of Irish experience. This is primarily a matter for board concern but has been included here as an operational issue because the ability to appoint high-quality women directors from in-house depends on the removal of 'glass ceilings' at all levels for women managers of ability.

The funding of UK pensions is a high-profile current topic of concern to both companies and all employees. Many UK occupational pension schemes remain seriously underfunded both in the public and private sectors and the chapter by James Borshell summarizes the Department of Work & Pensions' (DWP) important proposals for new regulation to replace the outworn traditional models.

During the recession the frequency of individual redundancies and redundancy programmes increased. Hopefully, the incidence of redundancy will diminish at least for the medium term, but the redundancy process will always be sensitive. In the closing chapter of Part Three, Henrietta Watchorn and David Whincup of Squire Sanders give detailed advice on how to manage each part of the process.

Part Four

For the final section of the book we set aside domestic issues which have come to prominence during the recent period of restraint and the 'lessons learned' – to cite the familiar phrase of those in authority who acknowledge failed policies or incompetent management without quite admitting responsibility. Looking beyond the domestic business environment, we re-assess risks in major developing and emerging markets.

In the opening chapter Gavin O'Toole examines political and operational aspects of environmental risk management in Latin America, followed by Carlo Gallo, now writing for his own independent consultancy Enquirisk, who revisits the root causes of business risk in Russia and future risk trends.

In the third chapter, James Pearson of Pacific Risk Advisors, another established Kogan Page author, reports encouragingly on the growing awareness and government action in addressing sustainability risk in China.

This year, Stephen Gill, our regular commentator on business in South-East Asia, discusses the development of a marketing and sales strategy for this disparate and challenging region where the opportunities are exciting but difficult to harness. It may be impractical to have a physical presence in each individual market and he advocates the employment of tried and tested development planning tools which he has found effective.

In the final chapter of the book I have again posed the question as to which emerging market offers the best balance today between opportunity and risk. This time, I invite readers to compare the risks in these markets with the opportunities for growth in more predictable advanced market economies by resuming or stepping up activities in the individual countries where their businesses are tentatively engaged or already have a footprint.

Acknowledgements

For each edition I am proud to express the publisher's and my personal thanks to the sponsors whose participation ensures that the book continues to prosper, and our appreciation this year is undimmed. Of course, publication is also not possible without the quality contributions of its authors, all experts in their fields and for some of whom this is the first time. My special thanks to those authors who write for the book regularly and who form an unusual species of 'pen pal'; and, once again, to Steve Fowler, Strategic Advisor to the Board of the Institute of Risk Management, for his Foreword.

As always, readers are encouraged to communicate direct with authors whose contact details are listed in the Appendix and I welcome correspondence on these or any potential new topics for the series.

Jonathan Reuvid
May 2014

PART ONE
Boardroom risk concerns and strategies

In today's global economy
the world is being remade
each and every day.

High performance. Delivered.

Opportunity is everywhere. We have the
experience, capabilities and resources
to help you seize it. Practical problem-
solving experience. Technology experience.
Industry knowledge. With approximately
266,000 employees serving clients in more
than 120 countries, we combine local
expertise with global know-how. That's
high performance, delivered.

consulting | technology | outsourcing

accenture

Beyond resilience: turning volatility and uncertainty into business opportunity

BEN CATTANEO, ACCENTURE FINANCE & RISK SERVICES

Organizations around the world have been compelled to operate in an environment of increasing volatility, uncertainty, complexity and ambiguity; hence the coining of the acronym, VUCA. Companies face the risk of sudden, severe events as evidenced by recent incidents in Ukraine, concerns over the eurozone and market wobbles stemming from a slow down of the Chinese economy. Sudden and unexpected events in remote locations can affect, and have already affected, company operations and supply chains.

This vulnerability extends to natural disasters. The eruption of the Eyjafjallajökull volcano in Iceland in 2010 affected air travel for weeks, sending some travellers on round-the-world routes simply to return home. 'Superstorm Sandy', which hit the north-eastern United States in October 2012, caused an estimated \$30–50 billion in property damage and effectively shut down most of lower Manhattan.[1] And in 2013, natural disasters in China cost the country \$68 billion, nearly double the total from the previous year.[2]

New, previously unconsidered risks emerge all the time. For instance, cybercrime, which was essentially unheard of 20 years ago, now threatens large corporations and governments as well as individual citizens. The shift to contract manufacturing – often conducted in offshore locations – can expose companies to reputational as well as operational risks, as evidenced by the recent collapse, accompanied by horrendous loss of life, of a manufacturing facility in Bangladesh.

There is a growing understanding that, over time, even the most risk-aware organizations can experience low-probability, high-impact events. These occurrences

– commonly called 'Black Swan' events after Nassim Nicholas Taleb's (2007) book – can fundamentally change businesses and even entire industries. Companies typically have measures in place to respond to such events under the banner of 'resilience'. These include business continuity and crisis management, disaster recovery and emergency response.

Accenture believes that traditional resilience management is often inadequate to deal effectively with extreme events. Such efforts are too often overly tactical and not integrated with other core risk management activities. We think that even fewer organizations actively prepare themselves to benefit from the upside of extreme events by embracing volatility and uncertainty. We believe that companies should consider addressing these shortcomings.

There is evidence that some organizations are already starting to do so. In Accenture's *2013 Global Risk Management Study: Risk management for an era of greater uncertainty*, a survey and interviews with risk executives at 446 organizations around the world, we found that leading companies, which we call 'risk masters', comprising 8 per cent of surveyed companies, are more focused on strategic and emerging risk than their peers. As will be seen, these firms are more likely to integrate resilience programmes into core risk management activities.

Where traditional resilience management often falls short

While recognition of the changing nature of risk is growing, few organizations are truly resilient, let alone able to benefit from acute events. In our view, there are a common set of deficiencies with traditional approaches to resilience which are summarized below.

Development of resilience initiatives by non-core business functions

Most business continuity management programmes are developed and managed separately from companies' core business operations, and most plans are tactical, rather than strategic. As a result, they are often focused on important but lowest common denominator items such as availability of spare office space and laptops. Conversely, when crisis management and business continuity plans are developed by business stakeholders – for instance, those leading key producing assets or managing supply chains – critical risk exposures are often uncovered and resilience can be improved. For example, a key supply chain choke point may be identified or an opportunity may become clear should certain types of risk events occur.

Disconnect from financial metrics

Few resilience programmes link risk exposures to cash flows and financial metrics, even though these elements are heavily exposed to the impact of highly disruptive events.

This can, therefore, lead to an underestimation of crisis impacts or an overestimation of what is important to the business. Stress-testing and financial simulations, much like those carried out in the banking sector, can help overcome this deficiency.

Lack of integration with other risk activities and functions

Business continuity and crisis management are not typically central to enterprise risk management (ERM) programmes or similar functions. In some cases, they are only loosely connected. This creates a 'pre-event bias' as the role of risk management is skewed towards forecasting and implementing controls to mitigate events before they occur. Nonetheless, risks can manifest themselves in spite of the best planning, and this ignores other types of uncertainties, as seen in Figure 1.1.1.

FIGURE 1.1.1 Event categories

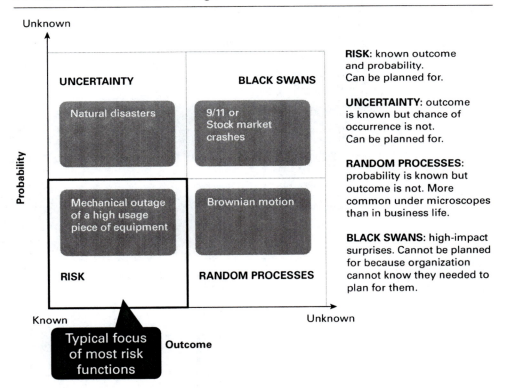

SOURCE: Accenture Risk Management, October 2013

Taking a new approach

We believe that resilience management can be just as important as other aspects of risk management. When a business integrates the management of acute events and

FIGURE 1.1.2 Resilience maturity framework

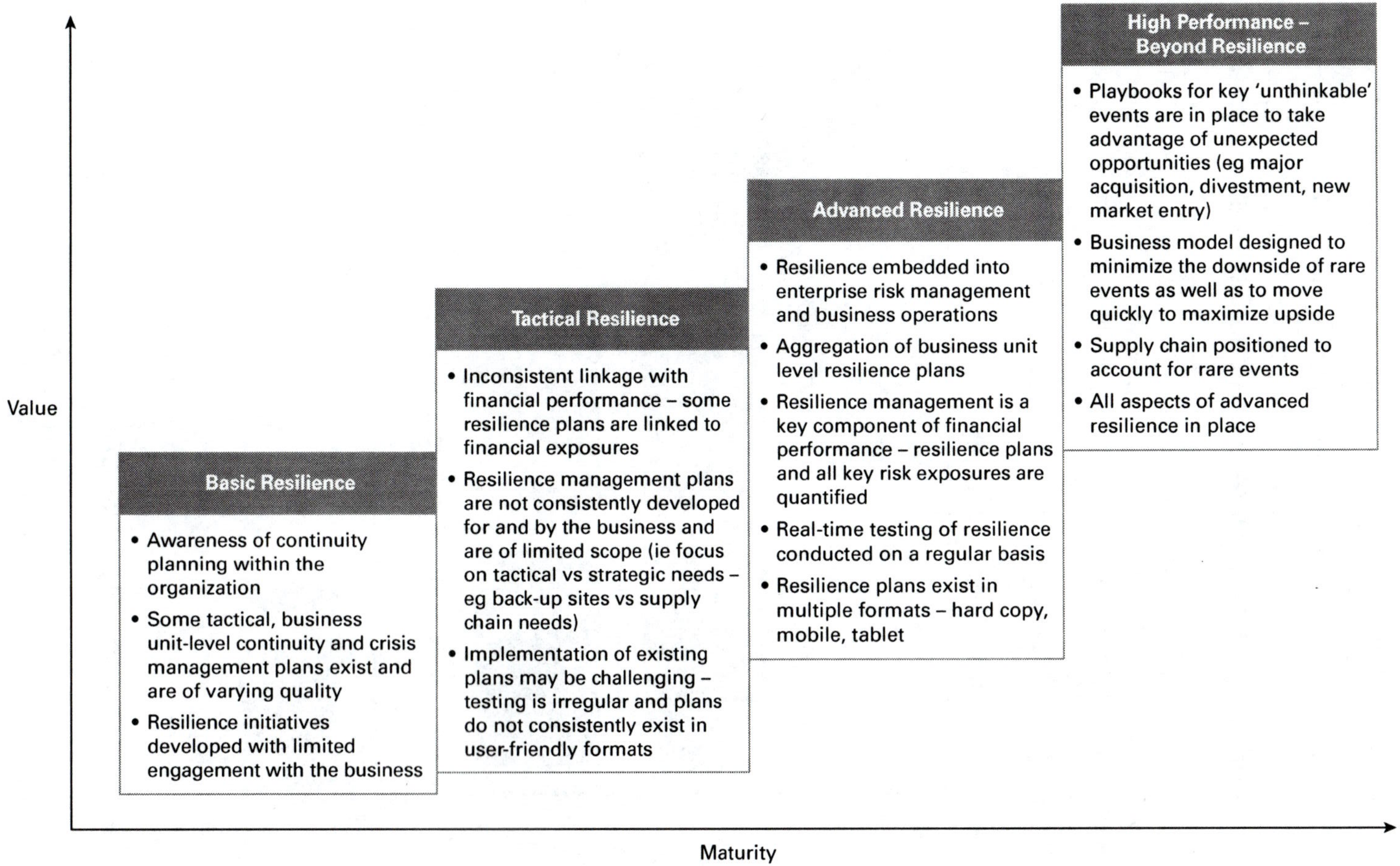

Basic Resilience

- Awareness of continuity planning within the organization
- Some tactical, business unit-level continuity and crisis management plans exist and are of varying quality
- Resilience initiatives developed with limited engagement with the business

Tactical Resilience

- Inconsistent linkage with financial performance – some resilience plans are linked to financial exposures
- Resilience management plans are not consistently developed for and by the business and are of limited scope (ie focus on tactical vs strategic needs – eg back-up sites vs supply chain needs)
- Implementation of existing plans may be challenging – testing is irregular and plans do not consistently exist in user-friendly formats

Advanced Resilience

- Resilience embedded into enterprise risk management and business operations
- Aggregation of business unit level resilience plans
- Resilience management is a key component of financial performance – resilience plans and all key risk exposures are quantified
- Real-time testing of resilience conducted on a regular basis
- Resilience plans exist in multiple formats – hard copy, mobile, tablet

High Performance – Beyond Resilience

- Playbooks for key 'unthinkable' events are in place to take advantage of unexpected opportunities (eg major acquisition, divestment, new market entry)
- Business model designed to minimize the downside of rare events as well as to move quickly to maximize upside
- Supply chain positioned to account for rare events
- All aspects of advanced resilience in place

Value

Maturity

SOURCE: Accenture Risk Management, October 2013

disruptions across the organization with an integrated view of risk categories and exposures, it may be better positioned to protect its ability to grow and achieve its objectives. We call this 'advanced resilience'. The most forward-looking practitioners of risk management, however – the companies we call 'risk masters' – are seeking ways, not just to respond and recover from acute events, but to gain competitive advantage from them. They are looking to go 'beyond resilience'.

The maturity model seen in Figure 1.1.2 illustrates our view of the various stages of maturity that resilience programmes often take.

Advanced resilience

Overcoming common deficiencies in resilience programmes involves integrating resilience within ERM and the core business. This consists of accepting that not all types of risks can be forecast and creates a risk management function that can encompass the many dimensions of risk, as well as the concept of uncertainty. These organizations can deal effectively with both types of events, as illustrated in Table 1.1.1.

TABLE 1.1.1   Risks from uncertainty

Risk	Uncertainty (illustrative examples)
Strategic risk	Natural disasters
Market risk	Price collapse
Credit risk	Politically-driven country default
Operational risk	Loss of critical systems
Reputational risk	Reputational event

We have identified three components critical to this approach:

1 *Leadership*. In advanced resilience, senior management is fully engaged and plays an active role in setting the resilience agenda. This involves the elements of:

   a. Preparation: roles, responsibilities in a crisis or acute disruption event are clearly assigned, understood, and rehearsed by all parties.

   b. Communication: clear communications to all audiences takes place before, during and after crisis events. These organizations have communication strategies for all stakeholder groups and use both traditional and social media to communicate.

   c. Action: once a crisis event occurs, leadership has access to needed information and is empowered to take quick, decisive action.

Part of the leadership role involves setting pre-defined parameters around what constitutes a crisis or significant event. 'Risk masters' establish clearly defined loss limits, and action plans may be triggered by certain situations, such as the loss of access to a specific market, an event that removes a critical process, or an acute supply chain disruption.

2 *Positioning*. High-performance practitioners closely integrate risk management and business continuity planning into ERM programmes. The reverse is true, as well; ERM criteria and risk profiles can help support risk management and business continuity plans.

Comprehensive resilience programmes are closely aligned with overall company strategy and financial performance. For example, there is a clear understanding of what assets are to be protected in the event of a crisis event or acute disruption. This strategy drives resilience planning, and the impact on cash flow and other financial metrics also features heavily in plan development.

In practical terms, this means that, while the risk function may facilitate the development of crisis management and business continuity plans, these plans are developed for and by the business. Just as the business owns risks, business units may be seen to lead planning and testing of resilience measures.

This also involves quantification of critical aspects of the business, using financial metrics such as cash flow, earnings and gross margin-at-risk. Finally, advanced performers are able to aggregate business unit plans up to the enterprise level, just as they would do with other core risk management processes.

3 *Execution*. Advanced companies innovate when it comes to plan execution. They use technology to monitor events and identify issues, and they engage in scenario-neutral planning to simulate various events and outcomes. High performers also use real-time stress tests to help identify discrepancies between plan assumptions and how things would play out in case of an actual disruptive event. Finally, advanced performers ensure that plans exist in multiple formats, including tablet and mobile devices. Gone are the days when crisis management and business continuity plans existed only in thick, hard-copy binders and folders.

High performance: going beyond resilience

We believe there are significant opportunities for companies to prepare themselves, not only for the downside, but for the upside of extreme events – akin to becoming 'antifragile', to use another term coined by Nassim Nicholas Taleb (2012). Achieving this level of readiness can entail moving from advanced resilience to a much higher state of integration and readiness.

Beyond resilience: components

No matter where the organization is on the spectrum of preparedness for unforeseen occurrences, there are a number of initiatives that can help companies take advantage of opportunities presented while protecting themselves from potentially damaging events. These include:

- *'Unthinkable Upside' playbooks*: companies can prepare plans and options not only to restore operations and recover lost business, but also to potentially take advantage of major events.

  These might include mergers, acquisitions, or accelerated entry into new markets in the event of a supply chain disruption, natural disaster or political upheaval. For example, a global manufacturer may wish to have strategic acquisition plans in place in the event that a sovereign default would dramatically lower asset prices in a particular country for strategically-relevant acquisition targets.

- *Business model reconfiguration*: a more comprehensive understanding of the potential impact of extreme events may lead some organizations to optimize their portfolio of businesses. Some lines of business may be deemed too sensitive to the potential impacts of a rare event, or have properties that do not expose them to sufficient upside in the midst of volatility or the manifestation of such events. Armed with a better feel for these exposures, the organization may then be able to reconfigure its business to make it more robust to uncertainty and volatility.

- *Reposition of supply chain*: an assessment of key suppliers may reveal overconcentration in some areas within the industry. This may mean that the company and/or its peers are over-reliant on one supplier, or that too many suppliers are clustered together geographically. For example, companies buying semiconductors and hard drive components in Thailand suffered severe disruptions in 2011 when flooding knocked out many major suppliers. Those with such insights can then reposition their supply chain so that they might gain market share from competitors in the face of unexpected events.

CASE STUDY   Going beyond resilience: an example

A major US retailer asked Accenture to undertake an assessment of their resilience needs, and design and implement a solution. We developed a framework keyed to the firm's corporate mission and enterprise risk strategy, and provided support in establishing programme governance, facilitating risk assessments and rolling out a resilience strategy across the business. This included processes and operational guidance for a '24/7' emergency operations center that supports retail stores across North America.

When Hurricane Sandy hit at the end of October 2012, the retailer was positioned to go 'beyond resilience' by being both aware of existing risk and equipped to understand uncertain events occurring in and around their retail outlets. The firm was able to directly and proactively leverage information gleaned from a posture of situational awareness into the most effective 'Notify–Assess–Respond–Recover' actions. This revealed an opportunity to serve their customer base more effectively. Emergency management and crisis management teams deployed resources – both personnel and equipment such as power generators – with speed and precision. As a result, most of the retail locations knocked out in a swath of 10 eastern states had reopened their doors in less than 48 hours.

A subsequent financial analysis revealed that revenue for the affected stores rebounded so markedly that the resulting associated revenue was greater than what would have been anticipated under normal conditions by several million dollars (see Figure 1.1.3). The analysis showed an unexpected revenue spike immediately prior to the storm's landfall, as customers flocked to the stores to purchase water, batteries and other essentials. By reopening stores following the storm's landfall more quickly than its competitors, not only was the retailer able to continue to earn revenues, but very likely enhanced customer loyalty and trust by being there for their customer base in a time of great need.

FIGURE 1.1.3 Hurricane Sandy: impact on sales

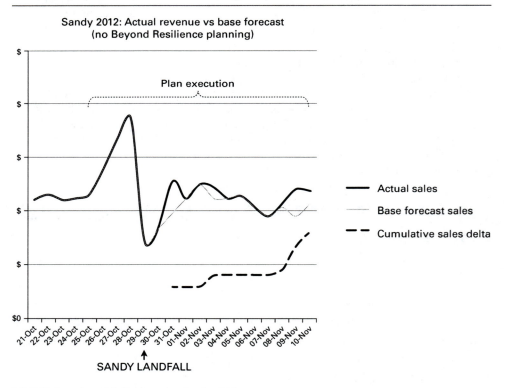

SOURCE: Accenture Risk Management, October 2013

Conclusion

We believe that organizations could benefit from exploring a new approach to volatility, uncertainty, complexity and ambiguity. Rather than simply plan to protect themselves from the impacts of such events, companies might consider embracing these features to create opportunities. Before being able to do so, however, many organizations may need to first enhance existing resilience processes by treating them as a key component of core risk management. Organizations that are able to do so can better prepare themselves for success, not only in spite of, but because of, what the future throws at them.

Notes

1 How hard did Hurricane Sandy hit manufacturers?, Ilya Leybovich, 6 November 2012, Thomasnet News [online] http://news.thomasnet.com/IMT/2012/11/06/how-hard-did-hurricane-sandy-hit-manufacturers/

2 Costs of natural disasters in China surge to $69 billion. Reuters, February 24, 2014 [online] http://www.reuters.com/article/2014/02/24/us-china-disasters-idUSBREA1N0JW20140224

References

Accenture (September 2013) *2013 Global Risk Management Study: Risk management for an era of greater uncertainty* [online] http://www.accenture.com/Microsites/risk-management-research/2013/Pages/the-report.aspx

Nassim Nicholas Taleb (2007) *The Black Swan: The impact of the highly improbable*, Penguin

Nassim Nicholas Taleb (2012) *Antifragile: Things that gain from disorder*, Penguin

Managing business disputes through mediation

BENNETT G PICKER, STRADLEY RONON STEVENS & YOUNG LLP

Introduction

When companies do business together there is always the potential for a dispute. A dispute may arise from disappointment, frustration, unreasonable demands, or even a legitimate misunderstanding. Regardless of the nature of the dispute, parties frequently have a difficult time resolving their differences in direct, party-to-party negotiations. Failing a resolution, disputants typically resort to litigation or arbitration and lose any ability to control the outcome. In addition to substantial risk, parties engaging in litigation invariably experience high costs, substantial delays, enormous distractions and the potential destruction of valuable business relationships.

Mediation defined

In contrast to the substantial risks and costs of litigation, mediation offers the potential for controlling the outcome of a dispute and developing real-time solutions. Mediation is a non-binding process that employs a neutral third party (the mediator) to facilitate negotiations in an effort to reach a mutually acceptable resolution. The process is:

- flexible;
- voluntary;
- confidential;
- informal;
- non-binding.

In mediation, the parties never relinquish the power and responsibility for resolving their disputes and maintain control over the outcome.

How mediation works

A mediator works with disputing parties to assist them in communicating, defining objectives, clarifying issues, resolving misunderstandings, assessing strengths and weaknesses, and exploring underlying interests. Ideally, mediation seeks to focus not only upon the parties' legal rights, but also upon their underlying business interests, needs, goals and objectives. As a consequence, in mediation, parties can craft a business solution that would be unavailable in litigation or arbitration where there is a declared 'winner' and 'loser.' Moreover, as the process can be convened in weeks or even days, the process invariably permits the parties to avoid the high costs, delays and distractions of litigation after which, regardless of the outcome, neither party perceives they have truly 'won'. In mediation, the parties are free to engage in creative problem-solving, restructure agreements, preserve their relationships and work together to explore creative business solutions.

Mediation and adjudication (litigation and arbitration) contrasted

While the benefits of mediation are substantial, litigation may be appropriate or even necessary in some circumstances such as, for example, where there is a need for an injunction or a need to obtain a precedent. The filing of a complaint in litigation or a statement of claim in arbitration may possibly be required in order to get the attention of the other party or to obtain 'discovery' concerning the underlying facts. However, disputants should keep in mind that the only information necessary to engage in settlement negotiations is that which is required to make an informed business decision. Moreover, any dispute that is amendable to a negotiated resolution is suitable for mediation.

Table 1.2.1 summarizes the differences between mediation and adjudication (litigation or arbitration).

How a mediator engages in facilitated negotiations

Parties to a dispute often find it difficult to communicate with each other once they engage in direct negotiations in an effort to resolve a business dispute. Anger, selective perception and advocacy bias often impair a party's ability to make objective assessments and responsible decisions about settlement.

A skilled and experienced mediator typically can overcome these obstacles to settlement and succeed in bringing parties together by trying to:

1 Manage the agenda.
2 Open lines of communication.
3 Clarify misunderstandings and frame issues.

TABLE 1.2.1 Mediation vs adjudication

MEDIATION	ADJUDICATION
• parties retain control over outcome and risk	• parties relinquish control to third party
• a neutral assists parties in defining issues and exploring interests and possible resolutions	• an arbitrator/judge listens to evidence and renders a decision
• need for discovery is often minimal	• discovery is often extensive, especially in common law nations
• process is private and confidential	• litigation not private, arbitration usually private, but award is sometimes made public
• parties are encouraged to communicate with each other directly	• all communications are through lawyer to tribunal
• focus is on all logically relevant factors including issues, interests, emotions, goals and relationships	• focus is narrow and limited to legal issues and a defined set of procedures
• joint sessions and individual caucus meetings are informal	• hearings are formal and evidentiary
• outcome is based upon perceptions and needs of parties	• decisions are based upon evidence and law
• parties often agree to mutually satisfactory resolution of dispute	• result makes one party a 'winner', the other a 'loser'
• issues in complex dispute can be telescoped into hours or days	• disputes often take years to resolve
• process is low-risk and cost-efficient	• costs are often very substantial

4 Probe fixed positions and underlying interests.

5 Make it safe for parties to be candid about their case and settlement positions in confidential private sessions with the mediator.

6 Explore new areas of discussion and creative solutions (thinking outside the box).

7 Act as agent of reality and help the parties make realistic assessments.

8 Make suggestions for mutually acceptable solutions, coach the parties on negotiating moves and float settlement proposals.

9 Ensure fairness in the process.

10 Place responsibility for the decision on the parties.

Credibility and trust are critical to a successful mediation. With complete impartiality and by actively listening to and reflecting back each party's positions and perspectives, a mediator can earn the trust of the parties. A skilled mediator will exhibit patience, professionalism and empathy for the parties' respective positions throughout the course of the mediation.

Preparing for mediation

Preparation is without question the key to obtaining a successful outcome in mediation. Regrettably, many parties spend insufficient time preparing for mediation. Perhaps it is the lack of familiarity with the process or the feeling that there is little likelihood of success. For some, there is a sense that because mediation is not binding, there is no downside. Of course, there is a downside to insufficient preparation. It is the enormous loss of an opportunity that can enhance the client's business objectives.

The following is an outline of key issues and concerns that should be addressed to maximize the likelihood of a successful outcome in mediation.

Exercise due diligence in selecting the mediator

The employment of a highly skilled and experienced mediator is critical to the success of mediation. Especially in a substantial dispute, a mediation advocate should engage in due diligence to assess the skill, experience and style of a particular mediator candidate. In addition to collecting the kind of data available on the internet, a mediation advocate should speak with other persons who have employed a potential mediator.

Identify and involve client representatives

It is important to encourage the participation of a decision-maker with full authority to make resolution decisions, even if this person does not have personal knowledge of the underlying facts at issue. Including the decision-maker enables the client to shape the impact that any outcome may have on the business goals and objectives of the client. If a party representative is articulate and persuasive, his or her statement directly to the other side can be far more powerful than any advocacy statement by counsel.

Develop a negotiating plan

Whether parties are engaged in a 'pure dollars' dispute or a more layered, complex controversy, counsel and the client should prepare a negotiating plan in advance of the mediation. All too often, parties lose a significant advantage in mediation as the result of having thought only about their end goals. Many mediations begin with the parties taking extreme positions and expressing an unwillingness to bid against themselves. In these circumstances, counsel should consider the advantages of making the first credible move. Even a small move, if credible, may enable the mediator to meet with the other side and gain significant concessions. Negotiation studies establish that the party making the first credible move can gain an advantage, referred to as 'anchoring and adjustment', by setting a recognizable benchmark from which settlement options are developed.

Determine whether information exchanges are necessary

Gaps in information present one of the principal reasons that disputes fail to settle in mediation. Especially in the early stages of a dispute, it is important that parties understand the essential basis of claims and defences including, in particular, the basis of alleged damages. It is difficult for parties to change their assessments on a real-time basis when this important information is conveyed for the first time in mediation. Accordingly, a mediation advocate should encourage the neutral to promote an efficient exchange of such information.

Prepare arguments supporting legal positions and settlement positions

A mediation advocate should develop an overall theme and prepare arguments supporting the merits of claims or defences with the same dedication as when preparing for trial. In addition, the advocate should also develop reasons why the other side should be willing to move to a 'reasonable' settlement proposal. Here, the advocate's goal is to persuade the other side to consider his or her client's proposal.

Prepare a confidential written statement to the mediator in advance of the mediation session

Regardless of whether the mediator asks for a confidential submission, a mediation advocate can obtain a significant advantage by submitting, in an informal letter, a confidential written statement summarizing the client's various litigation positions, including its rebuttal positions. A confidential submission also offers an opportunity to address the underlying issues, concerns and questions that often drive settlement decisions as much or even more than the litigation-risk analysis. Counsel should consider addressing issues such as: timing; linkage to an unrelated issue or dispute; strategic issues; personal relationship issues; need for privacy; internal company issues;

suggestions concerning process; suggestions concerning substantive resolution; and any other factors which may favour or present barriers to resolution.

Prepare a concise 'opening statement' for the joint session

Mediation advocates frequently say that there is no need for a joint session as the parties already understand each other's positions, or that excessive advocacy in a joint session will set the parties even further apart. While there are some instances that call for dispensing with a joint session, joint sessions usually have a number of advantages. For the mediator, a joint session offers an opportunity to go over the ground rules, and to obtain from each party a commitment to listen respectfully and to engage in good-faith negotiations. For the mediation advocate, a joint session offers an opportunity to have the other side's decision-maker hear the client's arguments, often for the first time, in a manner unfiltered by the other side's own counsel.

Make an objective litigation-risk assessment

A good mediation advocate owes a duty to his or her client to make a realistic assessment of the risks and costs of litigation. In advance of the mediation, an advocate will serve the best interests of the client by considering the only responsible benchmark for settlement decisions – comparing what might be achieved in settlement with the legal and business consequences of the litigation alternative.

Explore potential for creative solutions

Many mediation advocates bring their litigation perspectives to mediation and focus almost entirely upon issues of fact and law. Many also engage solely in 'distributive' bargaining where they exchange monetary offers and demands in an effort to 'divide the pie'. As a consequence, these mediation advocates and their clients fail to capture an opportunity to create value. In contrast, an advocate should encourage his or her client to engage in 'integrative' bargaining and take a more collaborative approach to mediation in an effort to create value in the negotiations.

Prepare a draft settlement agreement

Mediators will insist, at the very least, that upon reaching a mutually acceptable resolution, the parties enter into a binding 'term sheet' on all key issues. This document is essential to avoid a subsequent disagreement about the settlement terms and to avoid the possibility of later remorse. Mediation advocates should bring a settlement agreement draft covering the key economic and non-economic issues that need to be addressed in the event the dispute is settled in mediation.

Preparing for mediation requires an approach vastly different from the path an advocate takes when preparing witnesses for trial. At the same time, mediation advocates can maximize the potential for successful outcomes by employing the same level of dedication and professionalism as when preparing for trial.

Deciding whether or not to settle

Assuming parties to a business dispute are acting in good faith, mediation presents both sides with an opportunity to control the risks and costs of litigation and to achieve a binding settlement. However, too often parties do not seize this opportunity as they are incapable of making responsible settlement decisions due to a number of factors. Accordingly, parties should make every effort to consider the following when engaging in settlement discussions in a mediation.

Listen carefully

Due to the underlying frustration or anger which business executives typically experience in commercial disputes, party representatives in mediation often do not listen carefully to the other side. Often due to distrust, party representatives typically devalue information received from the other side regardless of the veracity of the statements being made or the strength of legal positions being advanced. It is imperative that decision-makers make every effort to put aside their frustration and anger and listen carefully to the other side's perspectives concerning a dispute. Among other things, new information learned will enable a party to make a better assessment of their risks in litigation should the parties fail to reach an agreement.

Make good assessments

Party representatives frequently make poor assessments about their risks in litigation or arbitration for reasons mediators refer to as 'cognitive biases' or 'cognitive barriers'. Among them are the following:

- *Advocacy bias:* most decision-makers and their counsel overestimate the likelihood of success in litigation as they spend a substantial amount of time identifying their strengths but pay insufficient attention to possible weaknesses. One recent study at the Harvard Program on Negotiation concludes that it is almost impossible for an individual with an interest in the outcome to make a completely objective settlement analysis.

- *Selective perception:* parties' assessments are often skewed by this phenomenon which is the tendency not to notice information that contradicts prior beliefs.

- *Assimilation bias:* party representatives often exhibit the tendency of individuals to see or hear only that information that favours their position. Victims of assimilation bias often behave as if the adverse information had never been presented to them.

- *Cognitive dissonance:* this bias refers to the fact that it is psychologically uncomfortable for individuals to consider data that contradicts their viewpoint. Disputants and attorneys tend to resolve conflicting information by justifying their own conduct, blaming others, and downplaying or ignoring conflicting data.

- *Endowment effort:* this cognitive barrier refers to the tendency to overvalue things in which one has a property interest (homes, cars, personal property and even the value of claims in dispute).

Perhaps Winston Churchill said it best: 'Where you stand depends upon where you sit'. As a matter of human nature, it is only normal for a party's or counsel's assessment to be skewed by the above and the many other cognitive barriers which affect judgement. However, in order to make a responsible settlement decision consistent with the interests of the client, disputants and their attorneys should make every effort to overcome the cognitive barriers that may impact sound judgement.

Make responsible settlement decisions

After listening carefully, making as objective a litigation-risk analysis as possible and fully exploring the parties' respective interests, parties ultimately will have to decide whether to accept a settlement in mediation or be subjected to the risks and costs of litigation. In making this decision, parties often focus upon what they want, what they need, what they believe is fair and right, and what they believe to be true. Of course, even litigation will not establish the 'truth'. Given the fact that jurors often decide cases based upon their own life experiences, and that judges can either make mistakes or make decisions based upon compromise, courts do not determine the 'truth' – they can only offer the parties a 'court truth'. Accordingly, parties should recognize that the benchmark for making a responsible settlement decision is to compare, at the end of the mediation process, the settlement on the table with what the real-world consequences are likely to be if the dispute does not settle (including risks, costs, relationships, distractions, interruptions in business, and publicity).

Businesses make a profit from the product they manufacture or the services they deliver, not from litigation. Parties to a dispute, therefore, should recognize that in order to reach a settlement agreement, it is necessary to compromise and to abandon settlement expectations that may be based upon the potential best outcome in litigation.

The landscape of mediation

While modern-day mediation dates back to the late 1920s with the advent of mediation of industrial relation disputes, mediation of commercial disputes did not become a widely recognized process until the late 1970s in the aftermath of the Pound Conference of 1976 (a historic gathering of legal scholars and jurists brought together to discuss ways to address popular dissatisfaction with the US legal system). This conference profoundly influenced and transformed both Alternative Dispute Resolution (ADR) and the US legal system. A few years later, the widely read book written by Roger Fisher and William Ury in 1981, entitled *Getting to Yes*, promoted the 'win–win' solutions obtainable in negotiations and mediation as the result of interest-based bargaining. In addition, in the 1980s, the movement for 'tort reform' prompted many corporations to embrace mediation in the search for faster, better and cheaper solutions. Many organizations, including particularly the International

Institute for Conflict Prevention & Resolution (CPR), promoted new pathways to institutionalize mediation in corporate contracts, court systems, and internal law firm and corporate cultures. Over time, most US court systems have included mediation programmes to assist in the resolution of disputes.

While modern-day mediation was initially a US phenomenon, many nations have since fully embraced mediation as a part of the culture of dispute resolution, including Canada, the United Kingdom (prompted by the Woolf reforms in 1999), Australia and New Zealand. In 2008, the European Union Mediation Directive required member states to promulgate national laws incorporating mediation. So far, only Austria, Estonia, France, Greece, Portugal and Italy have complied with the EU Directive. While Italy has seen a very substantial increase in mediation, the process of mediation in most other European nations remains in its infancy.

Today, ADR institutions worldwide, from Hong Kong and Singapore to Buenos Aires, are promoting mediation. The International Mediation Institute, headquartered in The Hague, Netherlands, promotes education and training of mediators and also offers a list of screened ('certified') mediators for the benefit of users. The Centre for Effective Dispute Resolution (CEDR), headquartered in London, has promoted mediation in the UK and Europe over the past 20 years. In 2013, the International Chamber of Commerce (ICC) hosted a conference to mark its worldwide launch of new mediation rules. In Europe, large global corporations, including General Electric, Nestlé, Akso Nobel, Northrop Grumman, Shell and others, have led the way in demonstrating how mediation can lead to earlier results and risk avoidance.

Conclusion

Notwithstanding the above recent developments, the promise and potential for mediation is one that remains largely unrealized. Many countries throughout the world have little understanding of mediation. Even in nations where mediation is part of the culture of dispute resolution, the understanding of and buy-in for the process is not very substantial. In many law firms, a culture of litigation is embedded, due to the fact that litigation remains a large profit centre in large commercial law firms and the fact that change does not occur quickly in a profession defined by its traditions. In many corporations, only a very few have a sophisticated understanding of mediation. Nevertheless, given the substantial benefits of mediation, it is likely that the trend favouring mediation will continue to rise in years to come.

Corporate greed in the capitalist garden of good and evil

GERARD BLOOM, CHIEF UNDERWRITING OFFICER, FINANCIAL INSTITUTIONS, XL GROUP

Introduction

With financial institutions as key sources and distributors of wealth within our societies, risk management departments are placed right in the middle of the debate as to what extent greed can be a force for good or a malevolent and destructive influence. We consider how the culture of an organization has an overriding effect on individual behaviours, some public examples of unacceptable behaviours, and to what extent the risk management department is empowered to manage the risks from excessive greed and what risk mitigants they may utilize. Finally, we consider whose responsibility it is to regulate an organization's culture.

> Greed, for lack of a better word, is good. Greed is right. Greed works. Greed clarifies, cuts through, and captures, the essence of the evolutionary spirit. Greed, in all of its forms; greed for life, for money, for love, knowledge, has marked the upward surge of mankind... .
>
> Michael Douglas as 'Gordon Gekko' in *Wall Street*, 1987

'Greed is alright, by the way. I think greed is healthy...' (Ivan Boesky, 1986)

In the beginning, or rather, some time close to it in the second millennium BC, capitalism was created. And everything was fine; or at least for the most part, until the South Sea Bubble in the early 18th century. British investors in the South Sea Company and the Mississippi Company lost much of their investments after the inflated value of the stocks crashed. The British government was forced to intervene in order to stabilize the banking industry. In fact, the British government outlawed the issuing of stock certificates, a law that was not repealed until 1825.

However, perhaps the relevant lesson for today's investors was the Wall Street Crash in 1929. This followed inflated stock prices, often manipulated by investment bankers, brokers, traders and even the owners themselves banding together to the detriment of unsophisticated or merely unsuspecting investors. By 1932, nearly 90 per cent of value had been wiped off the quoted stocks. In only the first quarter of 1933, over 4,000 banks had failed in the United States. The Great Depression followed, as did the establishment of the US Securities and Exchange Commission (SEC) to prevent further crashes and the fraudulent practices that had infected the stock market.

Then on 19th October 1987, the New York Stock Exchange fell 22.6 per cent in a single day following the exodus of investors amidst vastly inflated stock prices and a rash of insider trading investigations by the SEC. The Federal Reserve stepped in to prevent the insolvency of some commercial and investment banks.

Further market crashes ensued – for example, the 60 per cent-plus drop in the Nikkei through the 1990s and early 2000s, and the 'dotcom' crash during which the NASDAQ lost 78 per cent of its value (March 2000 to October 2002).

Regulators increased in numbers and increased regulation followed, but the markets had moved on, developed, become inter-connected and inter-reliant. Multiple regulators of multiple markets sprang up to regulate increasingly complex financial markets, where the views of various key rating agencies became critical to investors and the operation of certain instruments. This inter-relationship and connectivity of financial instruments paralleled the development of increasingly complex financial instruments since the 1980s, the advancement and use of technology to trade those instruments and the breeding of sedentary – or at least unsophisticated – regulators.

Just a few years later saw the credit crunch of 2007, the sub-prime crisis and global economic recession. Corporate failures, banking crises, government bail-outs, eurozone near-collapse, debt crisis, government bail-ins... politicians and media alike turned to the 'greedy' bankers to allocate blame while restructuring and empowering their regulatory bodies to hold them responsible and charging them to ensure it would never happen again. Just like in the 1720s, and the 1930s, and the 1980s, but with one fundamental difference: the scandals which accompany the crashes have moved from centuries apart to decades apart to years apart; maybe even to merely months apart.

In the midst of all of this sits the bank's risk management department, previously the habitat of corporate semi-grandees close to retirement and whose main role was to ensure delivery of a semi-annual board paper. Now these risk professionals are often qualified to a higher standard than the regulators whose multitude of rules they seek to interpret, while attempting to measure and mitigate the dozens of operational risks, before they strangle and destroy the very same organizations being blamed for the onset of the crisis.

In his 2011 paper 'Fear, greed, and financial crises: a cognitive neurosciences perspective',[1] Professor Andrew Lo comments on how periods of unchecked greed eventually lead to excessive leverage and unsustainable asset-price levels: 'It is not surprising that there have been 17 banking-related crises around the globe since 1974, the majority of which were preceded by periods of rising real estate and stock prices, large capital inflows, and financial liberalization. Extended periods of prosperity act as an anaesthetic in the human brain, lulling investors, business leaders and policymakers into a state of complacency, a drug-induced stupor that causes us to take risks that we know we should avoid.'

If greed has driven the western civilized capitalism to its knees, how can it be a force for good in the corporate world?

'Culture eats strategy for breakfast' (Peter Drucker)

There is an assumption that a desire to make profit within an organization is a positive sentiment. That can of course vary depending upon the motives and ownership structure of an organization; however, even not-for-profit organizations still need to make money in order to fulfil their corporate objectives, for instance, the funding of good causes. The functionality of society implies that the creation of wealth is positive with social benefits accruing, such as the better health of the population, lower crime rates, increased living standards, and so forth. Conversely, the lack of wealth creation within society has negative effects on health, crime, etc. Of course, these are rather simplistic assumptions, taking no account of the methods of wealth distribution or the uses of wealth within society and their effects on social benefits.

When considering whether greed – let's call it the drive to make money – is 'good' within an organization, one should distinguish between an organizational culture of excessive greed (to the detriment of ethical standards) versus individual excessive greed leading to fraud and the wilful flouting of regulations. However, one person's ethics are not the same as another's, nor one organization's the same as another's; similarly, one society's ethics are not the same as another's, or indeed their politicians' and regulators'. The culture within an organization and the boundaries or behaviours acceptable within society vary according to the environment which we entrust to our politicians and regulators.

Our regulators, therefore, have the unenviable task of trying to distinguish between regulating the ethical practices of organizations and the behaviour of those working for them – the framework of compliance for the entity versus the entity's own framework for the staff it employs to satisfy its corporate goals, none more so than owner or shareholder demand for satisfactory returns on their investments.

CASE STUDY   Corporate fraud

Much has been written about the corporate scandals of **Enron** and **WorldCom**, two organizations where it could be argued that unethical practices were embedded within the corporate cultures. The former grew to the seventh largest company in the United

States in just 15 years and precipitated the fall of Arthur Andersen, a giant of the accounting world. Both Enron and WorldCom were mired in accounting fraud and caused a raft of self-reflection amongst regulators and lawmakers. However, the problem didn't just go away amidst a flurry of litigation and legislation. The recent scandal at **Olympus** has highlighted that fraudulent practices can still become embedded within even the most high profile of companies.

Michael Woodford, former chief executive of Olympus, went public after discovering a US$1.7 billion fraud. The board, having failed to end the cover-up, instead voted unanimously to fire him. However, possibly the biggest scandal of all has been the resultant lack of jail sentences for the former chairman Tsuyoshi Kikukawa, vice-president Hisashi Mori and audit officer Hideo Yamada; while the company was fined the equivalent of US$4.6 billion and shareholders lost around US$7 billion in value. The rationale given by the court was that, despite the executives all pleading guilty, they had inherited the frauds from previous managements and were not involved in the original decision-making. They didn't benefit personally from hiding the losses. The message seems clear: provided you don't originate the fraud or gain personally from it, the Japanese courts will accept that as mitigation for the organizational culture in which you operate. To many, that would appear to be a strange message and unlikely to benefit Japanese companies in the eyes of international business.

Such frauds can of course happen in any company in any country as illustrated by the three big European scandals in 2003: **Adecco** in Switzerland, **Ahold** in Netherlands and **Parmalat** in Italy.

Of course, one person's accounting fraud is another's misunderstanding. The last few years have seen a slew of US shareholder actions against Chinese companies who have filed prospectus documents offering shares in the United States. The litigation has been accompanied by adverse media, especially through the financial blogging sites in the United States. Unquestionably, there have been a few cases of misleading information and even outright fraud in order to lure potential investors. However, it is starting to become noticeable that the majority of the problems lie not in fraud, but in different accounting standards and the disclosures that accompany them. The debate switches to one of transparency of the differences between Chinese and US accounting rules, rather than one of wilful misdirection and misstatement. The courts, or the companies themselves, may determine that the investors in the offerings deserve some sort of recompense for any such alleged misrepresentation, but certainly US plaintiffs have not seen the size or number of settlements that they may have anticipated. Should we really be surprised that regulators from two completely different cultures on different sides of the world operate and regulate to different understandings of different accounting rules?

The culture of employee fraud

Then there are those cases of outright fraud. In the insurance world, when a dishonest or fraudulent act by an employee of an organization leads to a direct financial loss for that organization, or a third party to whom it is held responsible, we term it 'employee infidelity'. Often the employee will perform such an act for their own personal benefit, but sometimes they will do it for someone else's enrichment – a good cause (eg a sick relative, a charity), a political or terrorist organization, or indeed organized crime.

There is a natural presumption that there is a synergy between risk and reward when considering the types of dishonest acts that are committed, but a look at most justice systems will tell you a different story. The potential rewards from a violent bank robbery pale into insignificance compared with the more 'white collar' frauds – electronic theft, for example – and yet the judicial repercussions are generally inversed. According to PricewaterhouseCoopers in their *2011 Global Economic Crime Survey*, cybercrime now ranks as one of the top four economic crimes and reputational damage resulting from cybercrime is the biggest fear for 40 per cent of the survey's respondents; the potential rewards are tremendous, possibly millions of dollars or even tens or hundreds of millions, yet the discouragements to commit such acts remain less than walking into a rural bank branch with a sawn-off shotgun where the potential take may only be a few thousand dollars.

Employee fraud remains one of the cornerstone operational risks determined by the Basel Banking Committee, as does external fraud. Banks are required to model their risk scenarios and to mitigate such risks through the setting aside of capital or, in limited instances, the purchase of qualifying insurance. Banking organizations will all profess to have excellent operational risk models, sound identification and modelling of risks, and appropriate measurement and mitigation of risks. They may all be correct, but the culture of each of those banking organizations is different, particularly in relation to what are acceptable levels of risk, dependent, potentially, upon the rewards available for individual risk taking within an organization. Do shareholders recognize that the organizations in which they invest have a higher or lower appetite for risk? Potentially, this is recognized through a perception of investment returns – they accept that a desire for returns significantly above industry norms will naturally come at an increased risk. However, it is highly doubtful that they would accept that achieving those returns comes at a compromise of ethical boundaries. There is and should be a reasonable expectation of the regulators to ensure that the environment in which companies operate allows reward of superior risk taking while stifling unethical behaviour within such organizations. It sounds simple, but history shows that regulators and legislators have to travel through an ethical and cultural jungle.

The culture of the rogue trader

Various high profile cases of rogue trading provide good examples of the ambiguity between individual actions and the moral compass of the organization in which they operate.

CASE STUDY   Rogue traders

In 1995, the British trader **Nick Leeson** singlehandedly brought down Barings Bank. Leeson was a star trader in Barings' Singapore branch, making huge profits in the early 90s speculating on futures derivatives. However, Leeson was hiding his losses in a secret account. He was discovered after the Kobe earthquake sent stocks plummeting, counter to his latest and largest bet which revealed the extent of his cover-up. The £827 million loss wiped out 233-year-old Barings' capital and reserves, and the bank collapsed.

In 1997, **Yasuo Hamanada** was sent to prison for eight years for unauthorized copper trades which ended up costing the Sumitomo Corporation US$2.6 billion. For decades, Hamanada would have Sumitomo buy huge quantities of copper and store it for a while in order to create an artificial shortage of the precious metal, thus driving up demand, before releasing smaller amounts on the commodities markets at extremely high prices. In 1998, Sumitomo paid US$150 million to regulators without any admittance of knowledge or condoning the actions of its rogue trader.

John Rusnak was a foreign currency trader working for Allfirst, a US subsidiary of Allied Irish Banks (AIB). Rusnak had a trading limit of only US$2.5 million but by 2002 he was betting up to US$7.5 billion on currency movements. When US$691 million went missing, along with Rusnak, AIB called in the FBI. The subsidiary was sold in late 2002 and Rusnak served over seven years in prison.

In 2008, **Jerome Kerviel**, a trader working for Société Générale in Paris, cost the bank approximately 4.9 billion euros after making an unhedged arbitraged trade on European futures to the value of a staggering US$60 billion without the bank's knowledge. He was recently sentenced to three years in prison after he lost his appeal.

UBS lost US$2.3 billion in 2012 after rogue trading by **Kweku Adobli**, one of its investment bank traders. Adobli had traded in excess of authorized risk limits and booked fictitious trades to hide his true risk exposures. He is now serving a seven-year sentence after being convicted on two counts of fraud.

All of these rogue traders have one remarkable thing in common: bonuses aside, none of them did what they did for personal financial gain, or to harm their employers. All of them claimed that their corporate environment drove them to take greater risk, to create more profits. These organizations would of course strongly deny such allegations, and indeed have done; some may claim instead that, while risk taking is encouraged within a controlled environment, little may be done to control an individual who is intent on ignoring their trading limits and hiding losses from management.

Dr Hans Breiter, the renowned expert in cognitive neuroscience, conducted a study which found that monetary gain stimulates the same reward circuitry as cocaine in the human brain. Professor Andrew Lo comments that in the case of cocaine, we call this addiction, but in the case of monetary gain, we call it capitalism!

The pressure then reverts back to the rule makers; how far should they go to inhibit risk taking within an organization, to control the instruments they trade, to mitigate the consequences of potential 'bad apples'? Kerviel could have brought down Société Générale and Rusnak could have destroyed both Allfirst and its parent AIB; neither of those eminent organizations would possibly argue that they would have wanted risk taking to such an extent; that would be preposterous. Yet Leeson's actions did bring down Barings.

These examples all resulted from unauthorized and secret actions by employee traders. The shocking fact is that these are only a handful of real-life examples; there are countless more of them, some comparable in size, some much smaller, but many, many more exist and have not come to public knowledge.

The economist and philosopher John Maynard Keynes wisely once said that 'Capitalism is the astounding belief that the most wickedest of men will do the most wickedest of things for the greatest good of everyone'.

The culture of the Ponzi scheme

We've all heard of the Nigerian e-mail scam. Send someone $1,000 and get $50,000 back, or something like that. Only a fool would fall for that scam so the story goes, yet people do, time and again, so the scam repeats and multiplies and reinvents itself. The potential rewards are so huge in relation to the probable downside risk that greed submerges logic even in the most intelligent of victims.

Expand the scam to a gigantic scale, put in the centre of it the former non-executive chairman of the NASDAQ stock market and almost US$65 billion in missing funds (including fabricated gains) from investor accounts, and you have Bernie Madoff. Actually, the final net loss to investors may 'only' be somewhere between US$12 billion and $20 billion, but this is still the biggest known financial fraud in history. In sentencing Bernie Madoff, the judge commented that his crimes were 'off the charts' since federal sentencing guidelines for fraud only go up to US$400 million in losses.

The mechanics of the Madoff Ponzi scheme were very simple. Once Madoff had determined the appropriate return for each investor, false trading reports were created from false trades from a previous date, creating the amount of desired fictitious profit. If customer redemptions were required, then the monies would simply be accessed via a bank account from their and other investors' funds.

However, this was a multi-billion dollar wealth management business with virtually none of the major derivatives firms trading with it, or Wall Street firms investing in it, because the high-ranking executives in those firms had their suspicions that it was not legitimate. Additionally, the financial analyst Harry Markopolos informed the SEC in 1999 that he believed it was legally and mathematically impossible to achieve the gains Madoff claimed to deliver. He was ignored by the Boston SEC in 2000 and 2001 and, after presenting further evidence, by the New York SEC in 2005 and 2007.

Also, this multi-billion dollar investment business was being serviced by an accounting and auditing firm with only three staff, of which only one was an accountant.

Hindsight is always easy, but there were plenty of red flags for the regulators to have acted long before they did. In fact, not long before the scandal of Bernie Madoff, in 2008, the Bayou Hedge Fund founder and star trader, Sam Israel III, had been convicted of defrauding investors out of US$450 million (the net losses probably being closer to US$75 million) and sentenced to 20 years in prison (increased to 22 years in 2009 after absconding and faking his own suicide) following the 2005 collapse of Bayou.

In his outstanding book, *Octopus: The Secret Market and The World's Wildest Con*, the true-crime journalist Guy Lawson comments at the end that he is convinced that Israel is sincerely remorseful for his actions and regrets the losses suffered by Bayou's investors. The fraud started with a 'small' lie, a few hundred thousand dollars mis-statement in published investment returns in order that the few investors which Bayou had at that time would not withdraw due to poor performance. The fraud ballooned beyond imagination as the hole grew bigger and bigger; Israel and his conspirators were forced to create a complicit accounting firm to validate the returns, while new investors began a steady rush to the fund attracted by the steady and consistent published returns.

Sam Israel resorted to increasingly far-fetched and bizarre investment methods to retrieve the position – there was an underlying desire to make good to his investors, to recover the fraud, just like an unauthorized trader doubling down and risking everything. Eventually, he bet the house on a prime bank con ('Octopus' being the nickname for the secret bond market only known and open to a few 'lucky' privileged investors), the sort of which bore all the hallmarks of an inflated Nigerian e-mail investment scam. The rogue trader, Ponzi scheme fraudster, had fallen for the most basic of frauds though his own desperation and greed. Israel failed to recover the missing monies in time and suspicious investors demanded their investments back. Bayou collapsed amidst a failure to meet redemption requests and a raft of legal, regulatory and criminal investigations.

Israel apparently shares the belief with many commentators that such investment frauds and Ponzi schemes were rife prior to the 2008 financial crisis. Ironically, the collapse of the markets probably gave plausible explanation for similar funds to hide inflated returns amongst genuine widespread investment losses.

Ponzi schemes bring all the elements of capitalist greed together: unethical corporate culture, individual acts of fraud and the rogue trading addiction to bigger and bigger bets while concealing huge losses.

The role of the risk management function

Risk managers of large, complex organizations now have an unenviable role. Not only are they tasked with designing, implementing and monitoring a risk framework within the organization, but they have to keep abreast of the multitude of new regulations that are being spat out by our lawmakers in response to public demand to control the banks who led the global economy into its current crisis.

The Dodd–Frank Reform Bill – all 2,319 pages – was signed into law on 21 July 2010, six months before the US Financial Crisis Inquiry Commission submitted its report and well before economists developed any consensus on the crisis. Would regulators approve a drug before its clinical trials were concluded, or the air authorities adopt new regulations in response to an airplane crash before the accident investigation had been completed? Add the euro crisis and new capital requirements for banks and other financial institutions, and risk management departments are facing moving targets just to keep their organizations merely 'competent' in tackling operational risks.

The extent to which risk managers can influence the control of the culture of greed within an organization and the excessive (fraudulent) greedy behaviour of individuals within the organization is highly dependent upon the culture of the organization itself. Many organizations espouse their risk management functions, but behind the glossy manuals and organizational charts, corporate attitudes to them can be vastly different. There needs to be a sense of empowerment within the function, an ability to influence through monitoring of risks and mitigating of exposures; in other words, risk management needs to be embedded within the culture of the organization.

The risk management function cannot be expected to determine the organizational culture, but, once empowered, it can have significant influence on the implementation of controls to prevent fraudulent behaviours.

The euro crisis has brought an onslaught of increased criminal activity. This is not surprising in view of the high levels of unemployment in southern Europe, the squeeze on employee pay and destruction in value of staff pensions. With pay cuts and job insecurity the norm, the doors of the banks are left wide open for organized crime to walk through – providing a malevolent influence within the organizations themselves.

Dual controls, segregation of duties, remote and on-site audits, checks, controls and procedures all provide parts of the toolbox for the risk manager to mitigate the risk of an employee determined to commit fraud. The purchase of insurance may also provide some mitigation of risk and can be built into the operational risk model and capital pricing.

Insurance as a potential risk mitigant

Crime insurance, sometimes known as 'bankers blanket bond' or similar, is one obvious method of mitigating the effects of a determined fraudster. With the right conditions and appropriate indemnity limits, regulators have been known to allow some capital mitigation for operational risk for the purchase of such insurance.

However, crime insurance will rarely extend to the unauthorized trading loss – most insurers taking the viewpoint that such actions are the fundamental business risk of the banks themselves; the traders are there to generate profits and the controls need to be embedded within the organization to prevent undue business risk (breaches of trading authority) taking place.

Some of the larger banks do continue to purchase errors and omissions insurance (often referred to as professional indemnity insurance) for their liabilities to third parties arising out of the professional services which they provide (including trading services). However, following mis-selling of retail financial products, investment banking scandals, negligent investment advice and many more besides, the cost of such insurance is fast becoming prohibitive for some – going beyond the relative cost of capital mitigation.

Increased focus over the last two decades has been on directors' and officers' liability insurance, which covers the managers of an organization for their potential personal liabilities arising from them carrying out their roles. Some cynics have called this the insurance coverage for when failure has already happened and management needs to protect itself from resultant litigation. A more realistic sentiment may be that this insurance demonstrates the reality of our litigious world where directors and managers within an organization will now be held responsible for their actions to the owners of the business – the shareholders. Those actions may include the implementation of effective risk management controls and procedures; and could even include the decision to purchase or not purchase sufficient insurance.

Directors' and officers' liability insurance (D&O) is now viewed as vital for any sizeable organization, particularly if the entity wishes to be able to attract high-quality non-executive directors and senior staff. Increasingly, lawmakers have been keen to try to hold those running businesses personally responsible for the decisions they are taking. Therefore, while there will be no capital relief motive available for risk managers to use as justification for the purchase of D&O, it is undoubtedly a key mitigant for the management of risk.

Conclusion

Greed, or the desire to make money, is what drives capitalism in the corporate world. However, we, as the public, taxpayers, shareholders and as society, have a right to expect the implementation of reasonable controls to prevent an abuse of power, the success of unfettered greed over prudent capitalism.

Arthur Andersen's collapse highlighted the conflicts of interest that exist in auditors' relationships with their clients. New rules have gone only some of the way to mitigate the conflicts, but there is still a widely held view that the big auditing firms remain too powerful and are allowed to indulge in significant fee-generating ventures not linked to their core service.

Increasingly the onus falls largely to the owners of our financial institutions to regulate the culture in which the businesses operate. The sometimes controversial Eliot Spitzer rightly argued that 'shareholders have the right and obligation to set the parameters of corporate behaviour within which the management pursues profit'. Therefore, the shareholders need effective management within organizations to protect their interests. Primarily, this falls to the non-executive directors, and the last decade has seen a dramatic cultural change as to their role. Their roles are now regarded as specialists and experts, equally likely to be held liable for their (in) actions. They too rely on testing the organizations' second and third lines of defence, the risk management function therefore being critical to the protection of shareholders' interests.

Ultimately, it is vital to get the corporate culture right, and determine acceptable behaviours while still driving the desire to make money. As much as many would like, it is not possible to regulate culture per se. Individuals within an organization create and embed the culture and only the individuals can change it willingly, while regulators and lawmakers attempt to force it.

It may not be feasible for a risk manager to determine whether the risk culture of an organization is appropriate, but an organization can empower them to manage the framework within which they control the unacceptable risks facing the organization and its shareholders. History shows us that those risk managers who are not empowered, who are overridden by the culture of corporate greed, will find themselves isolated and impotent.

Note

1   Prepared for *Handbook on Systemic Risk*, edited by JP Fouque and J Langsam

Recent and expected changes to regulatory reform

**NEIL MACLEAN AND KATIE RUSSELL,
SHEPHERD & WEDDERBURN LLP**

Since the launch of the Employment Law Review in 2010, the Department for Business, Innovation & Skills has introduced an agenda for change within UK employment law.

The review, which is expected to last into 2015, centres around the government's commitment to address certain existing employment laws which have been criticized for being costly, time-consuming and overly bureaucratic. The aim is to tackle these concerns and achieve the government's vision for a 'flexible, effective and fair labour market', allowing businesses to expand, employ more people and encourage a positive effect on the economy.

Below are some details of the key reforms of 2013 and an explanation of changes due to come into force in 2014. These include: changes in tribunal litigation, family-friendly legislation, new TUPE regulations and developments regarding the calculation (and cost) of holiday pay.

Changes in tribunal litigation

New tribunal rules

Following a number of consultations, new Employment Tribunal Rules of Procedure came into force on 29 July 2013. The changes under the 2013 rules include:

- updated claim (ET1) and response (ET3) forms;
- a new initial sift stage (where a claim or response can be dismissed in full or in part); and

- a 'preliminary hearing' replacing case management discussions and pre-hearing reviews (to address any administrative or preliminary matters, including strike-out applications).

Tribunal fees

Coinciding with the implementation of the new tribunal rules was the introduction of tribunal fees.

Since 29 July 2013, claimants have been required to pay a fee at the time of bringing a claim (the issue fee) and a further fee once the claim has been listed for a final hearing (the hearing fee). The level of fee depends on the claim type and number of claimants. For example, for single claimants with claims for unfair dismissal, discrimination or whistleblowing, the issue fee is £250 and the hearing fee is £950.

A fee remission scheme was introduced to allow those on low incomes to be exempt from paying tribunal fees. The scheme tests an applicant's disposable capital, as well as their gross monthly income, to determine whether or not they are entitled to full or partial remission.

It is perhaps too soon to draw conclusions about the impact fees will have on the volume of claims brought. However, early indications are that the number of claims will reduce and, in line with the government's aim, fees will 'encourage people to think more carefully about employment tribunals and alternatives'.

However, the introduction of fees has been controversial and was challenged by both UNISON (in England), and law firm Fox and Partners (in Scotland) who have each applied for judicial review. The arguments supporting these challenges included: fees create obstacles to the exercise of individual rights granted under EU law; fees are discriminatory; and no consideration was given to the potential negative impact of fees on those with protected characteristics. The High Court initially rejected the UNISON challenge but this is likely to be appealed, with Fox and Partners' proceedings in the Scottish Court of Session on hold in the meantime. If the challenge is successful, and fees are found to be unlawful, the government has undertaken to refund all fees with interest.

Cap on unfair dismissal compensation

Previously, compensation for unfair dismissal was subject to a flat rate cap, regardless of how much the employee in question earned. From 29 July 2013, compensation for unfair dismissal is now capped at the lower of: (i) £74,200 (expected to increase annually in line with prices), or (ii) 52 weeks' gross pay, subject to certain exceptions, eg where a whistleblowing disclosure is made. This has been welcomed by employers, who are now better placed to frame the parameters of possible settlement discussions with employees, and to forecast litigation risk. However, this change has also been challenged, by employee advisors Compromise Agreements Limited. In their submission to the judicial review they argue that the new cap will disproportionately adversely affect older workers who they argue will take longer to find new employment and so suffer higher income loss, which they will not be able to recover. The outcome of this judicial review should be known in the first half of 2014.

ACAS early reconciliation (April 2014)

As part of the government's focus on increasing the efficiency of the tribunal system, mandatory conciliation of claims came into force on 6 April 2014. Claimants will be required to submit details of their employment dispute to ACAS who will then attempt to conciliate a resolution with the parties within a four-week period. During early conciliation the clock stops on any time limits. If an offer of conciliation is refused by the employer, rejected by the employee, or the parties cannot reach an agreement during these four weeks, ACAS will issue a certificate entitling the claimant to proceed with his or her claim.

Families and flexible working

2014 and 2015 are set to be important years for family-friendly employment laws. Reforms, brought in under the Children and Families Bill following the government's 'Modern Workplaces Consultation', are being introduced in line with the government's aim to encourage flexibility in employment relationships.

Flexible working (June 2014)

From 30 June 2014, the right to request flexible working will be extended to all employees who have 26-plus weeks' continuous employment (currently this right is only granted to parents and carers). The current statutory procedure under which employers are required to consider flexible working applications has been criticized for being bureaucratic. It will be removed and replaced with a requirement on employers to consider requests 'in a reasonable manner'. Employers will be able to create or amend their own procedures for dealing with flexible working requests, allowing for a maximum period of three months, subject to any agreed extension of time, in which to communicate its decision on the request to the employee.

Employers will still be able to reject requests on the existing statutory grounds (such as the burden of additional costs, detrimental effect on the ability to meet customer demand and planned structural changes) but should adopt a consistent approach to granting and refusing requests.

ACAS has produced a short, draft code of practice to assist employers in managing requests, which, along with accompanying guidance, should provide useful advice to employers.

Shared parental leave (2015)

A new right to shared parental leave is expected to come into force in 2015. The recently published draft regulations outline the proposals.

Under the new scheme, eligible mothers will still be required to take the first two weeks' of compulsory maternity leave and will receive corresponding maternity pay. However, thereafter, it is proposed that eligible employees will be able to share the remaining 50 weeks' leave and 37 weeks' pay. It is proposed that, in order to qualify, the mother and partner must have responsibility for caring for the child and must pass a two-stage eligibility test (a joint economic activity test which a parent/carer would need their partner to pass in order to access the system, and an individual test to assess whether they are eligible for shared parental leave and pay).

Leave can be taken either in a single block or in non-consecutive sections. Both parents must give their employers eight weeks' notice of their intention to begin shared parental leave, in respect of each period of leave (with a maximum of three notifications per employee). The total leave taken cannot exceed the joint allowance, and must be taken within 52 weeks of the birth. Mothers will be entitled to 10 'keeping in touch days' in respect of her maternity leave, and the government has stated that, in respect of shared parental leave, each parent is also to have 20 'keeping in touch' days, which are expected to be renamed.

Similar protections will apply to parents on shared parental leave, as apply under maternity leave eg protection of contractual terms and conditions and accrual of holidays. Ordinary paternity leave (consisting of one whole or two consecutive weeks' ordinary paid paternity leave, to be taken within 56 days of the birth or placement for adoption) will still be available, but only where shared paternal leave is not being taken. Additional paternity leave and pay is to be abolished. This new scheme will also extend to eligible adopters, prospective adopters and surrogate parents.

TUPE reform

Following a call for evidence and subsequent consultation on the Transfer of Undertaking (Protection of Employment) Regulations (TUPE), substantial reforms were expected to reduce the bureaucracy and apparent 'gold-plating' within the regulations. However, the new draft regulations (the Collective Redundancies and Transfer of Undertakings (Protection of Employment) (Amendment) Regulations 2014), which came into force on 31 January 2014, do not contain the extensive changes anticipated.

Service provision changes

One of the biggest proposed changes was the removal of the service provision change rules under which TUPE specifically applied to outsourcings, insourcings and other changes to service providers. This was to address the fact that these provisions were 'gold-plating', over and above the requirements under the European Acquired Rights Directive which TUPE implements. However, it was felt that removing the service provision change rules would have created unnecessary uncertainty for businesses. Therefore, the rules relating to service provision changes have survived.

Employee liability information

The requirement for transferors to provide 'employee liability information' to transferees in advance of the transfer has been retained (despite the public consultation proposing that it be dropped). Under the new regulations, this information will need to be provided to the transferee 28 days prior to the transfer, rather than the 14 days currently required. This new requirement will apply to transfers taking place on or after 1 May 2014.

Economic, technical and organizational (ETO) reasons

Another proposal which has *not* made it to the final regulations is the suggestion that a transferor wishing to dismiss transferring employees prior to the transfer, should be able to rely on the ETO reasons of the transferee (eg dismissing on the basis that a redundancy situation will be created upon the transfer).

However, a change of location of the workforce is now expressly included as a potential ETO reason entailing changes in the workplace. Dismissal for this reason will not be automatically unfair, but the usual fairness tests would still apply. This reform is helpful as TUPE transfers commonly involve employees relocating to a different office and under TUPE 2006 if an employee refused to relocate following a TUPE transfer (even to an office nearby) and was dismissed as a result, this dismissal was automatically unfair.

Other key changes include:

- *Variations to employment terms:* it will not be possible to vary employment terms if the sole or principal reason for the variation is the transfer, unless (i) the reason is an ETO reason (and provided the employee agrees to the variation) or (ii) the terms of the employment contract permit the variation. This is less restrictive than the position under TUPE 2006.

- *Collective agreements:* under a static approach, only terms of collective agreements which apply at the point of transfer will be transferred; terms which are agreed and come into force post transfer, which the transferee has not had the opportunity to negotiate, will not automatically transfer under TUPE. In addition, collective agreements will be able to be renegotiated one year after transfer, provided that changes are no less favourable to employees.

- *Redundancy consultation:* collective redundancy consultation will be allowed to begin prior to a TUPE transfer and this time will count towards the statutory minimum collective consultation period under the Trade Union and Labour Relations (Consolidation) Act 1992.

- *Micro-employers:* employers with fewer than 10 employees will be able to consult directly with employees, rather than being obliged to inform and consult with representatives as required by TUPE 2006. This will apply to transfers taking place on or after 31 July 2014.

- *Guidance:* improved government guidance on TUPE will be produced.

Hot topic for 2014: holiday pay calculations

One area in particular in which significant changes may arise in 2014 is in the calculation of holiday pay. A number of European cases have led to a widening concept of holiday pay.

In *Williams v British Airways*, the Court of Justice of the European Union (CJEU) was asked to consider how holiday pay of BA pilots should be calculated. It held that holiday pay should put employees 'in a position, with regards to remuneration, comparable to periods of work'. Therefore, in addition to basic pay, remuneration for 'all the components intrinsically linked to the performance of the tasks' should be taken into account in calculating holiday pay. In *Williams* this included basic pay and a taxable hourly enhancement for flying time. Genuine expenses did not fall to be included in holiday pay calculations.

With regard to overtime, under the Employment Rights Act 1996, only overtime which is compulsory and guaranteed is required to be included in holiday pay calculations. In the employment tribunal case of *Neal v Freightliner Ltd*, the claimant worked a standard 35-hour week and regularly worked an additional 12 hours of overtime. In light of the decision in *Williams,* that employees are entitled to normal remuneration during holidays including remuneration 'intrinsically linked' to the work done, the judge added wording to the UK Working Time Regulations to disregard the requirement for overtime to be compulsory and guaranteed in order for it to be included in holiday pay calculations. Therefore, the claimant's pay for the overtime which he worked regularly, but voluntarily, was required to be taken into account in his holiday pay for the minimum four weeks' holiday provided under the Working Time Directive. This decision is being appealed.

A key decision in this area will be the decision of the CJEU in *Lock v British Gas* regarding whether commission should be included in the calculation of holiday pay. The Attorney General (AG) delivered his opinion that when calculating holiday pay for a worker who receives both basic pay and sales-related commission, both elements should be taken into account. The AG stated that the decisive criterion in determining what should be taken into account in the calculation of holiday pay is whether there is an intrinsic link between the components of remuneration paid and the performance of tasks under the employment contract, with a degree of permanence.

The CJEU is not obliged to follow the AG's opinion (but often does). If the CJEU rules that sales commission and similar payments are to be included in holiday pay, this could have a significant impact on employers. Organizations could potentially be liable to their workers for underpayments of holiday pay dating back to 1998, when the Working Time Regulations were introduced.

Conclusion

Employment law in the UK will continue to change through 2014 and into 2015. The next UK parliamentary elections take place in the spring of 2015. In anticipation, all of the main political parties will articulate their proposals for further labour law reform if elected to form the next government. It will be interesting.

Contracts which do not reflect the agreement reached

CHRIS JACKSON AND IAN TUCKER, BURGES SALMON LLP

Every business has key contracts whose performance can directly affect its operations or profitability. Some will be meticulously negotiated and drafted, often with legal input and advice. Others may be hurriedly recorded at a high level or concluded by the exchange of e-mail. However, in all cases, the business is likely to have a strong view about both what the parties' respective rights and obligations were and, separately, the benefits the contract was expected to bring.

What happens when, after the contract is concluded, it turns out that it does not have the effect expected or was based upon a false premise? Or when you pull it back out of the filing cabinet and it does not say what it is supposed to say?

At all times the possibility of an unintended liability or lack of profitability of a contract is a key risk for many businesses. This risk is normally assessed by management, both at the time of entering into a specific contract and in general against the ongoing viability of all the contracts that business has. That assessment must consider the extent of the impact of key contracts failing, the likelihood of a problem arising with such contracts, and the options and prospect for 'correcting' a contract which is not giving the expected results.

The risks posed

A contract which does not reflect business expectations can fundamentally redraw the rationale for entering it:

- A supply or sale simply may no longer be possible.
- A beneficial contract can be converted into a loss-making one with a potentially long-term commitment.
- The counterparty may behave unconstructively by seeking to vary the contract or claim that it was entered by mistake.

- If the contract is used for security or to underpin a credit rating, business financing can be impacted. Insurance arrangements might also need to be reviewed if cover is no longer adequate.

- In some cases (for example, financial services) contractual arrangements can be subject to regulation and must comply with certain legal obligations.

The likelihood and impact of such risks need to be assessed in connection with what action a business may wish to take on discovering that a contract is not as anticipated.

Problems can arise with key contracts at any stage. Although most significant 'mistakes' or false assumptions tend to come to light shortly after performance of a contract commences, it is not uncommon for errors to emerge months or even years after signature, perhaps when contracts are reviewed because business conditions have changed, new management has been appointed or insolvency threatens. A good risk policy is therefore to continue to recognize the possibility that any one or more key contracts could prove unreliable, particularly in adverse circumstances where parties revisit and review the specific terms of their contracts.

Objectives

If a serious risk is identified from a key contract, the business will wish to mitigate, transfer or avoid that risk (particularly if it is potentially a long-term contract or a contract which cannot easily be terminated). Commercial options may exist (such as additional insurance in some cases). However, the business may also wish to take a legal approach. Broadly this will aim at one of two options:

- *Avoid/terminate the contract.* In some cases the best option will be either to have the contract declared ineffective from the start (ie no effect is given to it and any steps already taken are unwound) or terminate any future obligations under it. This has the advantage of a clean break or a release from difficult (or potentially impossible) performance. However, the contract was presumably required for a reason and complete termination of it may leave the business without the supply or sale relationship for which it bargained. It will also often be impractical to unwind existing performance which may make a court unwilling to order that the contract was ineffective from the start unless a very prompt application is made.

- *'Repair' the contract.* If all parties, or the court, can be convinced that the contract contains errors (mistakes) then it is legally possible to amend it to read as it should have done. Courts are, however, cautious about such requests and can be hard to convince. Judges will start with the assumption that the contract means what it says and will need a good reason and evidence to depart from that position.

These options are, however, only available where the concern relates to the terms of the agreement or promises made in relation to it. If the contract is simply under-performing or failing to provide the benefits anticipated (even if those were known to the counterparty) no legal relief is likely to be available and the business will have to manage the risk accordingly.

The legal options available to avoid or mitigate the risks in these ways are outlined in the rest of this chapter.

The potential solutions

The most straightforward option, where all parties accept that there has been a genuine mistake is to amend the contract by agreement. Most contracts can be amended or novated (ie reissued) by suitable additional agreement. In some cases this will have to be in writing or in accordance with any variation clauses in the contract itself.

If this option is not available, a party wishing to change the contract can seek the court's assistance using one of the following arguments.

The contract has been amended by the parties' conduct

The way in which performance of the contract has been conducted may amount to a variation of its terms. Depending on the facts, if both parties have acted in a manner which differs from the wording of the contract it may be possible to show that 'objectively' they intended to vary it. This can fall foul of any term in the contract which requires variation in writing etc. In some rare circumstances it is also possible to argue that it would be unfair for one counterparty to go back on its statement about how it would perform the contract even if that differs from the strict contract terms (estoppel) – although this is usually only a temporary protection.

The contract should be read to have the intended effect

If a mistake is obvious, for example a simple typographical error, a court may simply read it with the mistake corrected. If the mistake is more complex, courts can still interpret any potential ambiguity in line with (objective) commercial intent or sense. Even where there is no ambiguity, in some cases it has been possible to convince a court that an error which is clear (in light of the exchanges leading to the formation of the contract) should be cured by simply reading an alternative construction. This is, however, rare and should not be relied upon.

The contract should be corrected to avoid the mistake

This is called 'rectification' and is available in two circumstances:

- *Common mistake* – both parties objectively meant the contract to say one thing but (due to drafting error) it says something different. The court will ask itself what an objective observer would have thought the intentions of the parties to be at the time the contract was entered. If:
  - the parties had a common continuing intention, whether or not amounting to an agreement, in respect of a particular matter in the instrument to be rectified;

- which existed at the time of execution of the instrument sought to be rectified;
- such common continuing intention to be established objectively, that is to say by reference to what an objective observer would have thought the intentions of the parties were; and
- by mistake, the instrument did not reflect that common intention;

then the contract can be amended. Subjective intentions (ie actual intentions which were not communicated) are not relevant. The court will only consider those matters which were communicated or can be objectively established from the conduct of the parties negotiating the contract.

In reality, this requires written contemporaneous evidence of communications between the parties where a clear intention or understanding is recorded. Most court applications brought for common mistake fail on this basis. What the parties would have intended if they had thought about it or had been properly advised is also irrelevant. Amendment this way is rare and businesses should ascribe a high risk to it.

- *Unilateral mistake* – the contract was entered by one party who was mistaken about its effect **and** the other party knew its counterparty was mistaken but did not mention it. The test for the court is:

- did one party erroneously believe the document contained or did not contain a specific term;
- was the other party aware of the omission or inclusion;
- did it realize that the omission or inclusion was due to the first party's mistake;
- did it fail to point out the mistake; and
- was the mistake a benefit to it (or potentially simply a detriment to the first party)?

Again, it can be difficult in reality to prove this. Written contemporaneous evidence is normally required both of the mistake and the other side's knowledge that it was a mistake. Amendment this way is also rare.

The contract is based on a misunderstanding or error, or its performance is impossible

Where a contract is negotiated and entered on the basis of a shared misunderstanding the contract can be struck down as a whole (from the beginning) for 'mutual mistake'. In effect, if the subject matter of the contract is misunderstood by the parties, no binding contract will ever have come into existence as there will have been no meeting of minds. An actual example is where goods were to be loaded onto a named ship leaving harbour on a specific day and, by coincidence, there were two ships of the same name leaving that day – the parties each assumed that the contract concerned different ships. Ironically the shared ship name was *Peerless*.

If the contract was possible, but intervening events have made it impossible, the contract may be terminated without fault for 'frustration'. An example is the booking of a named singer who died before the booking date.

These examples are very fact specific. Judges will seek to uphold a contract if at all possible and will be reluctant to accept that the parties were mistaken in what they agreed unless very compelling contemporaneous evidence is presented. Due to the increase in information access and professionalism, modern businesses rarely make fundamental errors over what they are contracting for.

One party was induced to enter the contract by untrue statements made by the other

Where untrue statements of fact are made (it does not matter if these are deliberate, negligent or accidental) and the other party enters the contract in reliance on them, the contract can be undone (from the beginning). The remedy is, however, discretionary and is less likely the longer the delay before the application is made. Actual (reasonable) reliance is required and has to be proved and the statement must be of the type which it would be reasonable to expect a counterparty to rely upon.

This is a relatively common cause of action, although it is very fact dependent and judges do take some convincing that active businessmen were genuinely induced to enter a contract by a statement from their counterparty. The statement relied upon must relate to facts (or in some limited cases, law) rather than predictions or benefits which might come from the contract. Unless the statement was made deliberately, this remedy may also be unavailable if the contract contains an 'entire agreement' clause or a 'no-reliance' clause.

The contract cannot be undone

If all else fails and it is not possible to 'undo' the contract, the business may be stuck with it or with substantial costs associated with terminating it. In such cases it may be possible to seek compensation for those losses from any professional advisors involved in drafting the contract if they have been negligent. Key to the success of any such claim will be evidence of the instructions given to the advisors and records of the advice they gave about the effect of the clause.

Choosing the solution

These solutions are all very fact dependent and can be difficult. When considering their options businesses should bear in mind:

- the need to act quickly once the mistake is revealed. Courts are much less likely to offer support if there is a delay;
- the need to understand in detail how the mistake arose;
- the difference between a mistake about the nature of the contract or the underlying facts (which can potentially be corrected) and a mistake about

the benefits which might flow from it such as sales or profits or opportunities, etc (which is unlikely to be corrected); and

- the overwhelming importance of contemporaneous evidence, ie the need to recover written records and communications quickly and effectively and to provide these to the courts. Law firms can assist with this and specialist computing consultants can be retained for electronic document (eg e-mails) collection and processing. The need for such records should also inform the means of communication and extent of record keeping which businesses use in connection with entering their contracts.

Overall business risk

There is always a danger that contracts will not turn out to have the effect anticipated. This is true both in relation to the potential benefits which flow from them, and in relation to the legal terms included in those contracts. Businesses should not assume that the signature of a contract is risk-free in terms of its later performance.

Key practical issues

- Make sure that your intentions for the effect of a contract are communicated **in writing** to the counterparty during negotiation.

- If the counterparty seems confused or changes its position during negotiation, make sure your interpretation/view is clearly communicated in writing before signature.

- Legal advice can be protected from disclosure in future disputes. Make sure you and your lawyers are gaining the advantage of such 'privilege' during negotiations.

- If a contract does not reflect the agreement you thought you had reached, seek confirmation from the counterparty without delay. Do not ignore a contract error, 'just because things are going fine'.

- Keep records of negotiations, including in particular electronic records (e-mails etc), for the lifetime of the contract if possible.

Once errors have been identified in a contract, there are a number of commercial and legal steps which might be taken to mitigate or transfer that risk. The legal steps are all very fact dependent and are consequently uncertain to protect the business. In addition they will involve potentially substantial up-front costs to obtain, which may well not be recovered.

This should have a number of impacts upon corporate risk analysis, in addition to the obvious risk to profit or the benefit of the contracts placed, which may need to be reflected in:

- the level of insurance and company liquidity to maintain;
- how records are kept (and how long) and what resources to incur on record keeping;
- the means of communication (written/e-mail rather than just vocal) when negotiating contracts and the documents prepared (eg for board meetings) setting out the business's understanding of the deal;
- what resources to incur on professional advisors in connection with negotiating key contracts;
- the compliance risk where the business is required to enter and maintain certain types of regulated contract.

Inevitably it will be cheaper and lower risk to commit sufficient resources to ensure that contracts are correct and effective when signed.

PART TWO
Managing information and online risk

Managing business opportunities and information risks

MARTIN SUTHERLAND, BAE SYSTEMS APPLIED INTELLIGENCE

Introduction

So what does 'cyber' or 'the digital age' mean to you? It's likely to depend on who you are, where you sit in the enterprise and what you are responsible for. For boards and senior executives the digital age is often seen from two polarized positions: from the incredible range of new opportunities it offers to improve efficiency and open new channels to customers, or alternatively as a recognized threat that is not properly understood. This thinking is exacerbated by the frantic pace of technological innovation and its adoption, often by the business rather than IT, which is making just keeping up difficult.

This chapter is intended to demystify some of the opportunities cyber and the digital age offer. And it suggests how enterprises can better exploit these in a secure manner. We illustrate different challenging scenarios that BAE Systems Applied Intelligence has worked on with different customers. These demonstrate how cyber security can be exploited as an enabler rather than a blocker to the successful pursuit of business opportunities.

Organizations identify two key functions at the core of their ability to achieve business objectives and pursue strategy:

1 Opportunity management or 'enhancing the business': the ability to identify, pursue and win business opportunities that will provide revenue and grow the business and innovative means to deliver better service to customers and citizens.

2 Risk management or 'protecting the business': the need to wholly understand and manage the full spectrum of risk that is faced by an organization. For example, the ability to securely bid for business opportunities without other bidders being aware of your offer.

Further, the effective management of risks and opportunities is increasingly seen as:

- a vital competitive differentiator, helping organizations achieve success and resilience during difficult economic times; and
- a key factor in demonstrating distinctive organizational attributes to the market such as agility, integrity and trust.

This chapter is intended to support executives in enterprises with responsibility for risk. It will highlight effective tools that can help to ensure an effective balance between opportunity and risk. It also raises pertinent questions that risk officers can legitimately raise to the board in the event they feel there is imbalance in their enterprise.

At the heart of this chapter is an exploration of the interaction between opportunity and risk management and the potentially damaging effects of an inappropriate balance in this relationship. Finally we present four scenarios of emerging cyber-enabled opportunities that challenge existing models and question how these opportunities can be exploited securely.

Technological innovation continues to radically impact and change the way society and business interacts and operates. In the *Harvey Nash CIO Survey 2013*, 71 per cent cent of respondents believed that their organization had to embrace new technology or risk losing market share.[1] This chapter is a timely contribution on how risk officers can support their organizations to benefit from the opportunities these innovations present, but in a secure manner.

'Balancing' opportunity and risk management

We all live and work in a 'connected' world. Our business and personal domains are blurring and this has helped to create a bewildering growth in the potential opportunities available to organizations. But it has also significantly increased the risks they face. Reduced 'barriers to entry' have swelled the number of threat actors seeking to exploit this connected world to their own benefit.

Within the information security domain, both risk and opportunity management as well as the interaction between them is gaining increasing focus. For example, chief information officers have responsibility for safeguarding their organization's data with appropriate cost effective controls, whilst also enabling business activities to fully realize the opportunities this information offers.

Most mature organizations will have processes in place to manage risks and to identify and track opportunities. But how many ensure that the two processes are aligned and that appropriate engagement between risk and opportunity management exists?

Too much focus on business opportunity can expose the organization to levels of risk far in excess of stated tolerances. Too much focus on downside risk can create stagnation.

Between these two extremes is a balanced area of high performance. The components of the balance between opportunity and risk management are illustrated diagrammatically in Figure 2.1.1 which considers:

- *Schedule*: what is the urgency of exploiting the opportunity and if so what is the risk appetite in this situation? If timescales are short, does this increase the security risk to the organization?
- *Cost*: what is the cost of implementing controls for a certain security risk? Does this cost still make the opportunity financially viable? Is this cost considered acceptable in order to meet business strategy?
- *Scope*: what is the risk that the information to be used as part of an opportunity can be compromised? Can the integrity of this information be ensured as part of the opportunity?

FIGURE 2.1.1   The components of opportunity and risk management

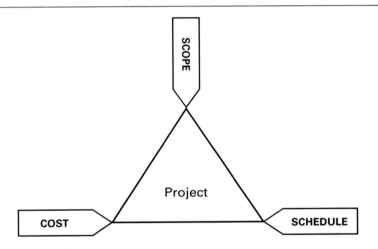

It is also important to note that once the opportunity has become 'business as usual', risk management should remain involved to ensure that the opportunity remains viable and that the security risk remains within the corporate risk appetite.

A common issue we see is that organizations base their risk management plan on a compliance-driven approach. This can be driven by operating in a regulated industry which focuses too heavily on impact over likelihood. Adopting this approach can impact opportunity management by creating areas of over-control whilst also exposing the organization to additional exposure by under-controlling other areas, as illustrated in the two graphs of Figure 2.1.2.

FIGURE 2.1.2   Expenditure vs risk

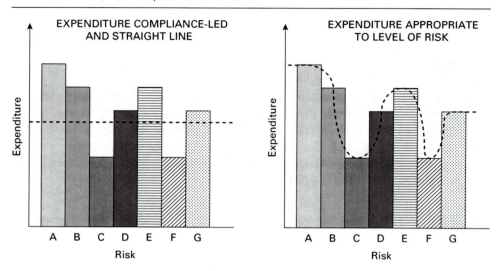

The left-hand chart shows restrictions of a compliance-led, straight line expenditure response, regardless of the risk. Areas above the dotted line are indicative of being over-managed and correspondingly those below are undermanaged. It's important to use an approach that ensures controls are appropriate and commensurate to the level of risk, as illustrated in the right-hand diagram. This approach can also ensure response is supportive of strategy and objectives and allows a more flexible approach to larger opportunities over smaller ones.

A second key issue we commonly see is enterprises not extracting the greatest value from existing controls. Risk officers increasingly demand not only a better return on their investment but also a way of better aligning risk management with enterprise strategy. This is shown in Figure 2.1.3. which illustrates the following:

1 Many organizations don't know how effective their security spend is.

2 Savings over one-size-fits-all approaches can be realized without increasing risk.

3 Risk can be reduced by focusing spend on those areas that are most significant.

4 The opportunity exists for an optimum trade-off between risk and spend.

FIGURE 2.1.3   Risk vs spend options

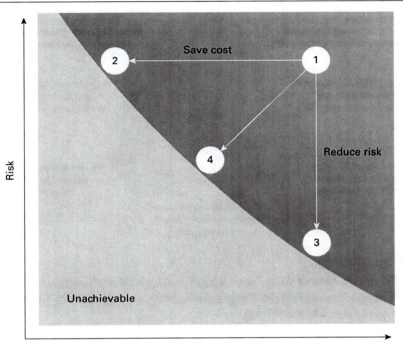

This lack of balance was identified in one organization where there was an expectation that any improvement of security controls would be at the direct expense of their ability to pursue opportunities. Through a risk assessment it was determined that existing controls could be better exploited at no extra cost and with positive impact in being able to pursue the opportunities – but now in a secure manner.

So far we have addressed how risk officers can look to derive the greatest value and benefit from their risk management controls. But how can risk managers ensure the wider enterprise is mindful of risk as it identifies and pursues opportunities?

A key foundation is ensuring that an appropriate risk governance structure is in place that recognizes the inter-dependencies between risk and opportunity. The associated costs of each are illustrated in Figure 2.1.4.

FIGURE 2.1.4 Interaction between risk, cost and opportunity

Risks identified early can be managed without compromising opportunity

Executive focus on pursuing opportunity while managing cost and risk

Piecemeal decisions often balance risk and opportunity poorly

Business cases for new projects often defer consideration of cyber risk

Information security often identifies risk late and in isolation from business

Weak costing of information assets and risks means they are ignored

Good risk management focuses spend where it is most needed

Successful recognition of these inter-dependencies and the adoption of a framework that ensures an effective and efficiently balanced risk and opportunity will help deliver significant benefits. These include:

- a risk management function that is aligned with and supportive of the wider business objectives and strategy;
- an ability to react in an agile and confident manner to new opportunities that arise as a result of technological innovation and new business models that will arise as a result; and
- a more resilient enterprise that is better prepared to react in the event of a cyber incident.

In the following section we outline four scenarios illustrating some of the risks and opportunities associated with emerging technologies being adopted in the enterprise.

Scenario 1: Mobile devices (BYOD/BYOT)

On the face of it there should be a clear-cut case for enhancing operational productivity by introducing personal mobile devices – bring your own device (BYOD) and bring your own technology (BYOT) – into the enterprise.

In reality, managing the opportunities and risks of personal mobile devices is far more complex. Typically it is rare that the business case has been fully considered, let alone documented. Correspondingly, there are usually no performance or risk indicators assigned to measure whether implementation delivers the predicted benefits of increased efficiency and productivity.

CASE STUDY   Delta Airlines

Delta Airlines announced they would be supplying tablets to all of their pilots. They will replace paper copies of flight manuals and maps with an estimated saving of $13 million per year. They will also replace a wide variety of personal devices that its pilots have already been using.

Similarly, we rarely find comprehensive risk assessments conducted for how the use of personal mobile devices might affect the overall risk profile of the enterprise. This is because the two primary drivers for their implementation commonly by-pass formal change management or assurance processes in place.

The first driver is from the bottom up. Staff will adopt practices and processes utilizing the increased functionality offered in advance of corporate policy. This exposes the enterprise to increased information security risk without the ability to leverage the opportunities offered. Driven from the top down it may have approval from the board but will only deliver benefit to a small group within the enterprise. Most commonly we see top-down initiatives introduced as 'trials' specifically to avoid controls in place to prevent such activity. These trials can last until the enterprise identifies a way for larger-scale deployment which again can result in increased information security risk in conjunction with a limited realization of the original opportunity.

The result is invariably a partial solution that delivers unsatisfactory results to both parties. Whilst it may be more difficult and take a bit longer, following the formal enterprise route for introducing new technology can allow for the key points identified above to be addressed.

Scenario 2: Using big data to secure the enterprise

A plethora of system monitoring and detection tools now exist to protect the increasingly diverse range of components that make up modern networks from a range of threats. These range from well-established anti-virus scans to specialized tools to detect evidence of cyber-espionage attacks attempting to evade detection. These tools offer unparalleled insights into the operations and performance of networks. And they also provide risk officers with the opportunity to deliver not just more effective network protection but also to enable the more efficient configuration and utilization of network resources.

CASE STUDY   McLaren Group

Automotive engineering and racing company McLaren Group places strategic importance on the protection of its information to exploit future opportunities for growth and innovation. McLaren uses a massively scalable platform to detect the underlying behaviours associated with sophisticated and bespoke cyber attacks, which typically go undetected and unfiltered by traditional methods that look for known attack signatures. This gives them assurance at a time when the threat landscape and the impact of new technologies on IT infrastructure management are constantly evolving.

Enterprises are increasingly seeking to move from a reactive to a more proactive security stance to identify, investigate and remediate attacks before lasting damage is done. In many instances current security information and event management (SIEM) tools are hampering an organization's ability to achieve this transition as they cannot effectively process the huge amounts of data now being collected from monitoring sources. Using big data in conjunction with effective and timely analytics can give risk officers a key tool in enabling this.

The ability to exploit the opportunities offered by big data is not without risks, which include:

1 Scale: the cost of capturing, ingesting, processing and storing the vast volumes of security alert data becomes prohibitive; and

2 Efficiency: unless correctly configured the sheer volume of security alerts generated, including false positives as well as low-priority alerts can overwhelm analysts. Furthermore, unless there is an aggregation tool in place, analysts will spend most of their time trying to connect the dots across different monitoring tools.

In order for risk officers to be able to truly embrace big data to help secure their enterprise it has to be done in a way which overcomes the risks highlighted.

Scenario 3: Connecting engineering and corporate networks

The practice of connecting previously disparate networks and systems together is becoming increasingly common in the enterprise. This scenario explores the opportunities and risks associated with connecting enterprise engineering and corporate networks, for example, industrial controls systems.

Control networks and corporate IT networks are connected to improve efficiency, in controlling industrial control systems, responding to notifications and for the business information that can be collected from these systems. Efficiencies are realized through greater automation, centralization and reduced associated overhead. The opportunity crosses into two other scenarios: remote diagnostics conducted centrally can then be transmitted to mobile devices held by field staff; and big data collected from the engineering network can be used to better calibrate and understand the performance of the system.

CASE STUDY   Saudi Aramco

In December 2012 Saudi Aramco, the national oil producer of Saudi Arabia, was the victim of a targeted cyber attack. The attack successfully compromised the corporate network with the intention of traversing to the engineering production network and disrupting oil and gas production. Whilst unsuccessful in preventing production it did wipe the hard drives of 30,000 computers on the corporate network.

Engineering systems have traditionally not been built with cyber security in mind. This was not an oversight or intentional omission – there was simply no need. The system was going to stand alone, use separate protocols and be operated by specialist staff. Security by obscurity was enough.

Connecting these systems to corporate networks that are connected to the internet has radically changed the risk profile that requires more effective risk management and mitigation measures.

Scenario 4: What the future might hold – the internet of things

A quick internet search for the 'internet of things' reveals that the number of 'smart' or embedded devices is expected to increase to 50 billion by 2020.[2]

CASE STUDY   Philips

Philips has manufactured LED light bulbs that connect to the internet and can be controlled via smartphone apps. It was quickly recognized by security researchers that the authentication method was vulnerable and could be easily compromised – allowing an attacker to switch lights on and off.

In many instances the opportunity to connect a device has trumped the risk of doing so and ensuring this risk is appropriately mitigated. This has a direct impact on the enterprise because many of these embedded devices are such commonplace items they are easily overlooked from an information risk perspective.

The opportunity, driven by user experience, is a seamless transition of data from and between devices and making it available to users regardless of their location or endpoint device. Incorporating this expectation into the enterprise clearly presents a myriad of risks. How long we have to work through these before it becomes reality remains to be seen.

In the meantime, risk officers have to recognize it is not enough to merely deal with the mainstream technologies. A finger on the pulse of emerging technologies is also required. There remain a range of options to combat this from a risk perspective. A common theme through these is placing greater onus on individuals to take personal responsibility for information security. An education and awareness programme with a focus on concepts and practices that benefit the enterprise but are transferable to employees' private lives would be a good place to start.

Conclusions and recommendations

Balancing information risk management and business opportunity management is difficult. It requires three different skillsets: understanding of business strategy; knowledge of the technologies involved; and an understanding of the current threats, as illustrated in the Appendix to this chapter. But the impacts of getting it right are significant and having an imbalance between the two can create significant damage. In summary:

- Ensure there is ownership of and responsibility for risk governance and its interaction with opportunity management at board level. This should then flow down the enterprise through management to the operational level, allowing lines of communication both up and down the enterprise.

- A way to ensure an effective balance is to conduct regular risk assessments and receive regular key performance and risk indicators between these assessments. This ensures the tolerance levels remain appropriate and that the corresponding control sets are commensurate with the level of risk faced.

- Where imbalances between risk and opportunities are detected, prompt remediation to address this will help ensure opportunities can still be pursued but in a secure manner.

- This normally entails recognizing information risk management is not an IT concern to be addressed through technical controls. Rather, it is a business function that must be informed by the enterprise strategy, priorities and risk appetite. It also has to be flexible enough to recognize that risk appetite may vary with each opportunity identified.

The pace of technological innovation and the rapid evolution of industrialized cyber threats makes it all the more important to ensure an appropriate mechanism for recognizing and responding to opportunity and risk is put in place. Paralysis in decision making can be the result, or worse still, the enterprise can expose itself to far greater risk whilst missing the opportunity to properly exploit the new industrial digital economy.

We have no shortage of examples where we have seen this situation develop, especially around the use of BYOD within the enterprise. Adoption can increase the level of exposure of critical information assets to associated threats. It also means the enterprise has to try to apply retro control, possibly harming its ability to pursue the opportunities these new technologies offer:

- Recognizing the opportunities and risks associated with new technology is key to helping inform the enterprise response. A risk governance framework that is not suitably empowered or is imbalanced will struggle to ensure the enterprise responds in a timely and relevant manner.

- Lack of awareness among executives and the board to the issues presented by new technologies should be rectified as quickly as possible. A lack of understanding or knowledge could result in the enterprise adopting the wrong position or delaying a response until it is too late.

The digital economy will continue to pose new information risks and business opportunities for all organizations. The ability for an enterprise to thrive in the uncertainty of this brave new world will be influenced by its ability to recognize the opportunities presented and pursue them in a secure way.

Notes

1 Harvey Nash CIO Survey 2013, www.harveynash.com/ciosurvey

2 http://blogs.hbr.org/2013/06/rethinking-security-for-the-in/

Appendix

Key questions for enterprise to ask in balancing risk with opportunity management. Is the enterprise able to show they...

Are clear who is responsible	• Who on the board is responsible? • Who explains the risk to them? • On what information will we make decisions?
Understand their cyber risk	• What information is most important to us? • What types of cyber risk do we care about? • How exposed are we to those risks?
Make active decisions on risk	• What is our appetite for risk? • Have we communicated this to all functions? • Are our resources deployed efficiently?
Plan for resilience	• Do we cover '10 Steps to Cyber Security'? • How will we know we are being attacked? • How will we thrive despite attacks?
Support strategic priorities	• Does our risk mitigation facilitate and enable growth? • Are our controls delaying or blocking progress? • Are we agile enough to exploit market opportunities?

And common answers that indicate risk and opportunity are not in balance:

Are clear who is responsible	Our IT department handles it
Understand their cyber risk	It is the same as everyone else
Make active decisions on risk	We do what we have to
Plan for resilience	We need to stop them getting in
Support strategic priorities	Security is a burden for us

Accountability for information practices

2.2

THEO LING AND JONATHAN TAM, BAKER & MCKENZIE LLP

Introduction

In May 2013, the Global Privacy Enforcement Network conducted its first 'Internet Privacy Sweep'. The internet privacy sweep is an annual probe of websites and mobile apps aimed at identifying privacy compliance issues. Nineteen privacy authorities from around the world participated in the inaugural sweep, including those from the UK, the United States, Canada, Australia, Hong Kong and Germany. The sweep captured over 2,000 websites of varying size and almost a hundred mobile apps. Focusing their efforts on how transparent organizations were about their information practices, privacy authorities found that 21 per cent of websites and 54 per cent of mobile apps had no privacy policies. Of the organizations that did publish privacy policies, many failed to disclose specific details of their information practices or did little more than regurgitate the wording of privacy legislation or make a high-level commitment that 'privacy is important to them'. Such compliance concerns were identified among half of the websites and the vast majority of mobile apps swept. Although it was not meant to be an investigation, various enforcement authorities took follow-up action during and after the sweep.

The sweep makes it clear that privacy authorities around the world are increasingly coordinating and enhancing their efforts to ensure that organizations are accountable for their information practices.[1] The penalties for failing to comply are serious. The UK Information Commissioner's Office recently fined a major technology company £250,000 after it failed to prevent a breach that put millions of users' personal data at risk. Across Europe, another major technology company has been subject to numerous fines (some set at the highest possible level locally) for failing to make proper disclosures in its privacy policy. Australia has handed out one of the highest penalties ever issued for failing to comply with anti-spam legislation (A$4.5 million), while the United States has imposed one of the highest penalties ever issued in the field of information governance generally (US$22.5 million).

Meanwhile, efforts are underway around the world to adopt and strengthen laws governing information practices. New Canadian anti-spam legislation will grant regulators the power to impose fines of up to C$10 million for sending commercial electronic messages without the consent of recipients. The EU's General Data Protection Regulation, expected to be adopted in 2015, will strengthen what is already one of the most comprehensive privacy frameworks in the world and will, if adopted in its current form, allow regulators to impose penalties of up to the greater of 100 million euros or 5 per cent of annual worldwide turnover for serious breaches. Other countries like Singapore, Malaysia, South Africa, South Korea and Trinidad and Tobago have recently adopted general data protection laws for the first time.

This shifting mosaic of increasingly prescriptive information governance legislation means that businesses cannot afford to take their obligations lightly. More and more, the financial costs and reputational damage associated with data breaches and regulatory investigations outweigh the costs of avoiding such incidents in the first place. This is especially so because regulators increasingly expect organizations to be accountable for their information practices. As the Chairman of the European Commission's data protection advisory group Jacob Kohnstamm noted, 'when looking at the bigger picture, you indeed can detect a trend that data protection and privacy rules across the world are getting closer to each other, for example with regard to principles of transparency and accountability'.[2] This chapter focuses on how organizations can succeed in becoming accountable for their information practices.

What is accountability?

Accountability is essentially the highest standard that an organization can achieve when protecting the personal data under its control. An accountable organization takes responsibility for its information practices, models its operations on best practices, and minimizes the risk that any information under its control is improperly collected, used, stored, communicated, disclosed, lost or stolen. Moreover, an accountable organization can demonstrate to regulators, business partners and consumers that its information practices successfully minimize compliance risks.

Ever since the OECD introduced the concept of accountability to privacy law in 1980 through its *Guidelines on the Protection of Privacy and Transborder Flows of Personal Data* (Privacy Guidelines), accountability has become a foundational principle for almost every jurisdiction with developed privacy legislation. In 2013, the OECD crystallized over three decades of discourse on accountability when it revised the Privacy Guidelines to include a section on implementing accountability. These revisions represent privacy authorities' consensus on the core aspects of accountability. According to this new section, organizations should have in place a privacy management programme that:

1 gives effect to the Privacy Guidelines for all personal data under its control;

2 is tailored to the structure, scale, volume and sensitivity of its operations;

3 provides for appropriate safeguards based on privacy risk assessment;

4 is integrated into its governance structure and establishes internal oversight mechanisms;

5 includes plans for responding to inquiries and incidents;

6 is updated in light of ongoing monitoring and periodic assessment.

This list emphasizes that accountability is based on having a proper privacy management programme, which is essentially the body of policies, procedures and practices relating to and surrounding the personal data under the organization's control. In this article, we use the term 'information governance programme' to emphasize that the scope of the programme may go beyond general data processing to include all information practices such as social media communications, digitizing records, bring-your-own-device (BYOD) policies and protocols, whistleblower hotlines, electronic marketing messages and so on. This broadened scope also aligns with the recent trend among lawmakers to enact rules governing big data, ie the collection and use of extremely large and complex volumes of data.

The section on implementing accountability goes on to explain that organizations should:

> Be prepared to demonstrate its privacy management programme as appropriate, in particular at the request of a competent privacy enforcement authority or another entity responsible for promoting adherence to a code of conduct or similar arrangement giving binding effect to these Guidelines.

This paragraph highlights the importance of being able to demonstrate to privacy authorities and third parties that an organization effectively protects personal data. As will be further elaborated below, to achieve this end, an organization must implement mechanisms that periodically collect evidence of the information governance programme's performance, and be prepared to furnish such evidence to third parties as appropriate.

Finally, the section on implementing accountability states that organizations should:

> Provide notice, as appropriate, to privacy enforcement authorities or other relevant authorities where there has been a significant security breach affecting personal data. Where the breach is likely to adversely affect data subjects, a data controller should notify affected data subjects.

This paragraph simultaneously describes a feature of accountable organizations and demonstrates why organizations should move away from reacting to their information governance obligations on an ad hoc basis. An accountable organization voluntarily notifies the appropriate authorities and data subjects when a data breach has occurred. However, where organizations have a legal obligation to report data breaches to authorities (such as in Austria, China and Germany), there is an even greater incentive for organizations to seek to minimize the risk of data breaches, ie to adopt an accountability approach to their information practices. Note that data breach notification requirements will only become more commonplace as lawmakers work on strengthening privacy legislation worldwide.

Achieving accountability

While the steps to achieving accountability will be different for every organization, there are three broad measures that an organization must ideally implement to be accountable:

1 Management must designate at least one individual who is responsible for the organization's information governance obligations and provide that individual with the support and resources to implement an information governance programme across the organization.

2 The information governance programme must be based on robust, detailed and tailored legal foundations and prescribe best practices for all individuals in the organization.

3 Evidence of the success and shortcomings of the information governance programme must regularly be compiled and reviewed with a view to updating the programme as necessary.

These elements are interrelated. An effective information governance programme cannot exist without management support and oversight. At the same time, an effective information governance programme implements mechanisms that result in the compilation of evidence of the programme's effectiveness, and such evidence assists management in gauging the organization's compliance risks and calibrating the resources required to maintain and enforce the information governance programme. The interplay among the three components is represented in the accountability framework illustrated in Figure 2.2.1.

FIGURE 2.2.1 The accountability framework

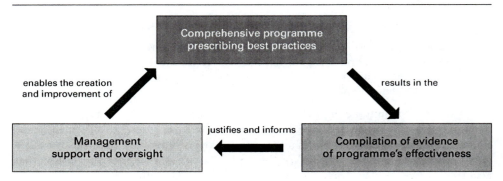

Accountability begins with executive responsibility and adequate support

To achieve accountability, it is crucial that an organization designate someone at the executive level who is responsible for developing and improving the organization's information governance programme. Doing so signals to third parties that the organization accepts ownership of its information practices and validates its commitment to legal and regulatory compliance.

However, it is not enough for an organization to establish a token privacy or legal department without providing it with the support and resources to implement effective policies and procedures. When deciding how much support to provide, organizations should bear in mind that implementing a strong information governance programme is generally less costly than taking an ad hoc approach to compliance obligations. Temporary and patchwork solutions fall apart when laws evolve, and the costs of managing data breaches and regulatory investigations can quickly spiral out of control. Meanwhile, an organization that establishes a comprehensive information governance programme that prescribes best practices can be confident that most changes in the law will not require substantial and costly modifications to its information practices.

A comprehensive information governance programme that prescribes best practices minimizes compliance risks

An organization's information governance programme dictates how every individual, group and system within the organization must carry out information practices. To achieve accountability, the information governance programme must be based on solid legal foundations that take into account all of the legal obligations to which the organization is subject. These legal foundations will be different depending on the organization's structure, scale and geographical presence, and the volume and sensitivity of the information under its control. The information governance programme must then prescribe practices that put these legal foundations into effect. For an organization to be truly accountable, the practices prescribed by the information governance programme must align with recognized best practices, which are those practices that are recognized by experts and regulators as minimizing the risk that information under an organization's control will be improperly collected, used, stored, communicated, disclosed, lost or stolen.

Thus, for example, based on principles found in most data protection statutes around the world, a strong information governance programme will include policies and procedures that adhere to and prescribe the following broad best practices:

Best practice in information governance programmes

The organization shall:

1 Maintain a personal data inventory that organizes personal data under the organization's control according to their sensitivity and keeps track of all of the data's essential details such as where they are stored and for what purpose(s) they are being used.

2 Maintain a privacy policy that outlines the organization's expectations, requirements, and responsibilities with respect to the collection, use, retention, storage, disclosure and transfer of personal data.

3 Maintain operational policies and procedures ensuring that specific information practices such as cookie use and online advertising are conducted in a compliant manner.

4 Conduct ongoing training and awareness programmes to promote compliance with the organization's policies, procedures, and other components of the information governance programme.

5 Ensure that administrative, physical and technical security safeguards are effectively put in place so as to minimize the risk of improper or unauthorized collection, use or disclosure of personal data.

6 Ensure that all agreements with third parties are consistent with the organization's policies, procedures, and other applicable components of the information governance programme.

7 Ensure that all notices and communications to data subjects with respect to their personal data are consistent with the organization's policies, procedures and other applicable components of the information governance programme.

8 Maintain public relations policies and procedures for receiving and responding to inquiries, complaints and requests from data subjects regarding the accuracy, use and deletion of their personal data.

9 Regularly monitor new technological developments to identify new processes that could improve the organization's information governance programme.

10 Maintain a system that allows the organization to identify and rectify data breaches in an expeditious manner.

11 Continuously verify compliance of members of the organization with the organization's policies, procedures, and other applicable components of the information governance programme.

12 Regularly monitor new developments from legislators, regulators and industry bodies, and determine how they may impact the organization's information governance programme.

To be accountable, an organization's information governance programme must also provide specific guidance on how its information practices are to be conducted. Developing policies and procedures that provide specific guidance can be challenging because there may be no relevant legislation governing the information practices at issue or because such legislation is of a very general nature. Take mobile apps for example. There is little legislation that specifically addresses the manner in which mobile apps are to collect, use or disclose personal data, although there are general requirements on data controllers to process personal data only for specified, explicit and legitimate purposes, to obtain affirmative consent to such processing, and so on.

To develop an information governance programme that provides specific guidance in the absence of specific statutory requirements, as a starting point, organizations should look to guidance documents published by regulators and industry bodies. Such guidance documents usually provide specific guidance with respect to specific information practices such as the development of apps, the use of cookies and online behavioural advertising. In some circumstances, failing to incorporate the best practices set out in these guidance documents can lead to enforcement actions. For example, regulatory and industry guidance documents consistently warn app developers not to collect personal data from a mobile device user's address book without the consent of the persons in the address book. In 2013, the Canadian Privacy Commissioner and the Dutch Data Protection Authority collaborated to investigate the developers of a popular mobile messaging app that, among other things, required users to allow the app to access their address books so that it could populate their chat lists. The privacy authorities of both countries determined that the app violated local privacy laws and required it to change its information practices.

In sum, organizations seeking to be accountable should look to legislation, regulations and regulatory and industry guidance documents as a source of best practices that they can integrate into their information governance programmes.

Accountable organizations regularly compile evidence and use it to improve their information governance programmes

Another defining feature of accountable organizations is that they are able to demonstrate that their information practices successfully minimize compliance risks. To achieve this end, an organization must implement mechanisms that ensure that it is regularly compiling evidence of the successes and shortcomings of its information governance programme. In the event of an audit, records of these reviews constitute the most readily available cache of documentation that can be used to demonstrate accountability.

Achieving accountability also requires regularly assessing the results of these reviews in a productive manner. Updates to an organization's information governance programme are necessary where the results indicate that significant compliance risks exist, such as where preventable data breaches or leaks have taken place. In addition, an organization should compare its information practices and safeguards against established benchmarks and those of similar organizations to determine whether and to what extent improvements to its information governance programme are necessary.

Conclusion

When considering how best to prepare for a future in which accountability is the global standard to which organizations are held, an organization should assess whether its policies, procedures and practices succeed in minimizing the risk of information under its control being improperly collected, used, stored, disclosed or lost. To achieve accountability, the management of an organization must commit to ensuring that its information practices minimize compliance risks and adhere to best practices. As part of this commitment, the organization must establish a holistic information governance programme that is based on detailed and tailored legal foundations and which prescribes best practices across the organization. When properly implemented, such a programme will provide the organization with robust evidence of the strength of its information governance programme. Incorporating these three elements will help organizations achieve accountability and engender trust among their business partners and consumers.

Notes

1 The term information practices refers to any activity that involves the collection, use, storage, retention or disclosure of information, as well as the manner in which such activities are carried out.

2 Comments made at the 34th International Conference of Data Protection and Privacy Commissioners (24 October, 2012).

Selling online: the EU Consumer Rights Directive

DORIS MYLES, BEN ALLGROVE AND STEVE HOLMES, BAKER & MCKENZIE LLP

Introduction

The consumer landscape for online sales in the EU is changing in 2014 with the entering into practical effect of the EU Consumer Rights Directive (2011/83/EU) (the Directive).

The title of the EU Consumer Rights Directive is slightly misleading. The original scope of the Directive when it was first proposed in 2008 was to create a uniform set of consumer rights across Europe, but its remit was reduced significantly during its negotiation stage due to failure to reach agreement across the various member states as to what those uniform rights should be. As a result, the final version of the Directive does not cover *all* consumer rights but instead principally harmonizes and introduces new rights for consumers when buying from a trader at a distance, for example, when buying online.

The Consumer Rights Directive replaces existing EU consumer directives on distance selling and doorstop selling. Each member state was required to publish national legislation to implement the Directive by 13 December at the latest. Those national laws (implementing the Directive) will enter into force on 13 June 2014 and will apply to contracts entered into after that date. The six-month gap between the publication of the legislation and the date it comes into force is to enable companies to update their online terms and conditions and sales processes to ensure that traders are compliant on the actual date the Directive comes into force.

Importantly, it is a maximum harmonization directive, and therefore member states must ensure that their national laws do not go further than the terms of the Directive.

In the past, online traders involved in cross-border sales to consumers across Europe were required to contend with very different national consumer laws for online sales in the EU, because the law was based on minimum harmonization approach.

It is hoped that this new directive will standardize consumer law requirements for online sales and make it easier for traders to sell good and services across Europe. However, as the Directive will be implemented in each member state by national legislation, member states will still be able to have some minor flexibility to adopt the rules in certain aspects.

Some industry sectors are outside the scope of the Directive, for example gambling, financial services and residential letting contracts, as they are subject to separate EU regulation.

What is a consumer?

The Directive defines a consumer as any natural person acting for purposes outside his trade, business, craft or profession. However, member states have the flexibility to extend the application of the Directive to legal persons who are not consumers, such as non-governmental organizations or small and medium-sized enterprises.

What are the key changes for online sales to consumers?

The key changes imposed by the Directive can essentially be broken down into three areas:

- information which must be provided by a trader to the consumer before and after a sale is made online;
- changes to a consumer's cancellation rights for a purchase made online; and
- prohibition of hidden costs.

What are the new information requirements?

The Directive requires a trader to provide certain information to a consumer before and after a sale is made. This information must be provided in a clear and comprehensive manner and in plain and intelligible language, as follows:

- *Cancellation:* the trader must inform a consumer before a sale of the consumer's right to cancel and withdraw from the purchase contract during the cooling-off period. The cooling-off period (called the 'withdrawal period' in the Directive) entitles the consumer to change their mind about the purchase, cancel the contract and obtain a refund. This right of withdrawal is entirely separate from a consumer's right to return goods if they are faulty. Failure to provide information about the cooling-off period will extend the cooling-off period from 14 calendar days to 12 months.

- *Returns:* traders must inform a consumer before a sale if the consumer must bear the postage costs of returning goods when the consumer cancels the contract during the cooling-off period. Failure to do so will mean that the trader has to bear the cost. Of course, many traders operate a 'free returns' policy and absorb this cost without passing it on to the consumer.

- *Pay button:* traders must make it absolutely clear to the consumer at what stage the consumer is entering into the contract with an obligation to pay by using a click button or similar function labelled 'obligation with an order to pay' or similar unambiguous formulation such as 'pay now'. This is to make it clear to a consumer exactly at what point they have an obligation to pay the trader and to avoid a situation where a consumer clicks a 'join us' or 'subscribe' button and fails to understand that at that point they are entering into a binding contract.

- *Digital content:* before a sale, traders must provide a consumer with information on the functionality of digital content, including applicable technical protection measures and any relevant interoperability with hardware and software of which a trader could reasonably be expected to be aware. Digital content means data which is produced and supplied in digital form, such as computer programs, apps, music, video or texts, irrespective of whether they are accessed through downloading or streaming or from a tangible medium.

- *Model withdrawal form:* traders must supply a model withdrawal form on their website and inform the consumer before the sale that the consumer has an option to use the withdrawal form if they want to cancel the contract during the cooling-off period. Importantly, the consumer is not required to use the form but can cancel the contract by making any other unequivocal statement to the trader confirming cancellation, for example a telephone call or e-mail. The provision of a model withdrawal form is a new requirement and the easiest way for a trader to provide a withdrawal form is to provide a link to a pop-up box which the consumer can complete and submit to the trader to confirm their cancellation. The Directive contains language that should be used for the withdrawal form.

- *Durable medium:* after the sale, a consumer must be provided with a confirmation of their contract in a durable medium. A new development in the Directive is that durable medium is defined as 'any instrument which enables the consumer or the trader to store information addressed personally to him, in a way accessible for future reference for a period of time adequate for the purposes of the information, and which allows for unchanged reproduction of the information stored'. Examples of durable medium are e-mails or texts, or secure personal accounts which remain accessible to the consumer.

Clear and comprehensive information

One of the important requirements of the Directive is that the consumer is able to fully read and understand the main elements of the contract before placing the order.

As a consequence, the Directive requires information about the main elements of the contract to be placed in close vicinity to the confirmation that is required from the customer to place the order. This obligation may require some traders to amend their websites to ensure that the customer is provided with the information at the right stage in the purchase flow.

Technical constraints in providing information

The Directive recognizes that in certain cases it will be difficult to clearly set out all the necessary pre-contractual information, for example, limited space on a mobile phone screen. In those situations, traders must supply some minimum information, such as the main characteristics of the goods or services, the identity of the trader, the total price and the right of withdrawal, and refer the consumer to another source of information, for example a link to the trader's web page or a toll-free telephone number where the consumer can access the remaining information.

What are the new cancellation rights?

There are new rights and requirements if a consumer decides to cancel their purchase during the cooling-off period:

- *Cooling-off period:* the right of withdrawal is now 14 calendar days. This is a no-fault right for a consumer to withdraw from the contract and seek a refund. If the goods or services that have been provided are faulty then a consumer has an entirely separate right to return the goods and seek a refund.
- *Refunds:* if a consumer cancels the contract during the cooling-off period, the trader must refund all payments including the price and any standard delivery charge paid by the consumer, within 14 calendar days of the cancellation date. However, a new trader-friendly provision in the Directive allows a trader to withhold the refund until it has received the returned goods or proof of postage from the consumer.
- *Digital content:* there is no cooling-off period if downloading has started but the consumer must have given prior express consent to start performance and acknowledged that by doing so, the consumer loses their right to cancel.
- *Return of goods:* the consumer is required to send the goods back to the trader within 14 calendar days of cancellation. As stated above, a consumer will be required to pay for returns as long as the trader has made that clear before the sale.
- *Diminished value:* traders can reduce the amount of the refund paid to the consumer for goods that have been returned by showing evidence of use by the consumer beyond normal handling to see if the goods are as expected. For example, it may be reasonable for the consumer to remove packaging in order to inspect the goods that have been ordered or to try them on, but it

would not be reasonable to use the goods in a manner that went beyond the type of inspection that a consumer would carry out if they were purchasing the goods in a shop.

When is there no right to cancel?

In line with the previous law on distance selling, there are various circumstances where a consumer will not have a right to cancel during the cooling-off period, for example if the goods supplied are clearly personalized or made to a customer's specification, or are sealed goods which are not suitable for return due to health protection or hygiene reasons, where the consumer has unsealed the product after delivery.

Similarly, where a consumer has ordered a service, and performance of the service has begun with the consumer's prior express consent and with an acknowledgement that there will be no right of withdrawal once performance has started, then there will be no cooling-off period.

One new provision in the Directive is that there is a difference in the ability of a consumer to cancel digital content during the cooling-off period. The Directive confirms that where digital content is:

- *not* supplied on a tangible medium, ie digital content is downloaded or streamed, then it is treated as a service and the consumer has no cooling-off period, subject to the same consent and acknowledgement provisions as for the supply of services; and
- if digital content is supplied on a tangible medium, such as a CD or DVD, it is considered to be goods and the 14 day cooling-off period will apply (unless the CD or DVD is supplied sealed and it is unsealed after delivery).

What hidden costs are prohibited?

Traders cannot impose hidden charges on a consumer and as a result a trader must seek express consent from a consumer for any additional payments in addition to the price paid for the goods or services. This covers:

- *Pre-ticked boxes:* traders cannot use pre-ticked boxes on a website where it results in a payment by the consumer. A pre-ticked box can still be used if the product or service is free, for example, a free newsletter.
- *Telephone calls:* traders cannot use premium rate telephone helplines. A consumer may not be charged more than the basic rate to call a customer service helpline or to discuss an order or problem with the supplied product or service. However, a trader can provide a different premium rate helpline for a particular additional service package provided that it is made clear to the consumer that it is a separate, paid-for service.
- *Excessive card charges:* traders are prohibited from charging consumers a fee for the use of a particular payment method where that fee exceeds the

cost to the trader for processing such a payment. For example, some traders have been criticized for charging excessive fees for processing payments made by credit card. If traders charge a booking or administration fee which does not discriminate between different payment methods then this is allowed under the Directive as this cost is just part of the overall price.

Are the new provisions in the Directive mandatory?

The provisions in the Directive are mandatory and consumers cannot waive their rights in a contract. Any attempt by the trader to change these rights in their contract with the consumer which results in a direct or indirect restriction of the consumer's rights under the Directive will not be binding on the consumer. Of course, if a trader wishes to give the consumer better rights in their contract, which go beyond the provisions in the Directive, then this is acceptable. For example, in the UK, many traders will give the consumer a much longer cooling-off period, for example three months.

How will the Directive be enforced against online traders?

The Directive provides that member states must ensure that there are adequate and effective national procedures to ensure compliance and member states must implement penalties that are effective, proportionate and dissuasive to ensure that traders comply with the Directive. It is not yet clear whether this requirement will result in any material change to the consumer remedies currently available.

Summary

Companies selling to consumers online in the EU should review their terms of sale and websites to ensure they are compliant with these new provisions when they come into force on 13 June 2014.

Consumer protection has become increasingly 'flavour of the month' at EU level, and national regulators in the member states are now more experienced and vigilant enforcers of consumer rights and consumer protection rules; alongside this, EU consumers are now more 'educated' in their rights and more confident in asserting them and challenging non-compliant traders.

Reference

Directive 2011/83/EU of the European Parliament and of the Council on Consumer Rights

The Systemic Risk Survey 2013

JONATHAN REUVID, HETHE MANAGEMENT SERVICES

Introduction

Every two years since 2009 the Bank of England conducts a survey, the Systemic Risk Survey, to identify risks to the stability of the UK financial system and publishes the results. The most recent 2013 H2 survey was carried out between 23 September and 24 October 2013 and published a month later. Participants included UK and large foreign banks, building societies, hedge funds, asset managers and insurers. The survey questionnaire is completed by executives responsible for risk management in each organization. This time 76 participants took part representing a 99 per cent response rate.

The survey focuses on four key questions:

- probability of a high-impact event;
- confidence in the UK financial system;
- key risks to the UK financial system;
- risks most challenging to manage as a firm.

The findings of the 2013 H2 survey, which was conducted at the time when the economy showed the first real evidence at macro level of its gradual recovery from prolonged recession, are of particular interest, although the Bank of England hastens to caution readers that the results do not necessarily reflect its views on risks to the UK financial system.

Probability of a high-impact event

The perceived probabilities of a high-impact event in both the short and medium term have declined steadily since 2011 at the height of the euro-currency crisis and again slightly since May 2013 when the previous soundings were taken. Only 7 per cent of respondents now consider the short-term risk as high or very high (6 per cent in May 2013) while 55 per cent consider it to be low or very low (50 per cent in May 2013).

The medium-term picture is broadly congruent. Whereas the same proportion of 24 per cent as in May 2013 considers that there is a high or very high medium-term risk, 16 per cent (3 per cent more than in May) now rate the risk as low or very low. Moreover, these results are reflected in respondents' own opinions as to whether or not the likelihood of a high-impact event occurring had changed over the previous six months. A net balance of 50 per cent thought that the short-term probability had diminished, against 5 per cent who thought that it had increased.

Confidence in the UK financial system

Overall confidence in the UK financial system has also increased markedly since the autumn of 2011 when only 15 per cent were very confident, 57 per cent fairly confident and 28 per cent not very confident. In the autumn 2013 survey, although only 19 per cent expressed complete confidence or were very confident, 78 per cent are now fairly confident of the stability of the UK financial system over the next three years while just 4 per cent remain not very confident. The survey confirms that a net balance of 28 per cent of respondents declared an increase in their confidence over the previous six months.

Of course, there is an inherently subjective element in these findings arising from the composition of the sample. Notwithstanding the traumatic effects of the global financial crisis, the severe threats to the stability of the euro (abated for now but still subject to medium-term concerns) and a succession of revelations of continuing bad practice, both domestic and international, among the joint stock banks, the survey demonstrates that the financial community has regained its self-confidence in sustainability. Whether or not that perception is shared by the wider business community or the public at large remains a moot point.

Key risks to the UK financial system

Respondents were next asked to identify the five risks which they thought would have the greatest impact, if realized, on the UK financial system. The relative frequency of the five most cited risks from the most recent survey and the five previous surveys is displayed in Table 2.4.1.

The supplementary question asked of respondents in the series of surveys was which of the nominated risks would have the greatest potential impact, and these findings are summarized in Table 2.4.2. The two sets of responses are complementary and need to be read together.

TABLE 2.4.1   Key risks to the UK financial system

	2011		2012		2013	
	H1	H2	H1	H2	H1	H2
Key risks						
Sovereign risk	66	76	79	94	76	74
Risk of an economic downturn	69	76	79	77	79	67
Risks surrounding the low interest rate environment	4	1	4	9	26	43
Risks around regulation/ taxes	32	38	40	34	39	41
Risk around property prices	31	16	21	14	25	36

SOURCE: Systemic Risk Survey 2013 H2, Bank of England
Units: % of respondents

TABLE 2.4.2   No 1 risk to the UK financial system

	2011		2012		2013	
	H1	H2	H1	H2	H1	H2
Key risks						
Sovereign risk	36	62	60	68	38	39
Risk of an economic downturn	36	13	16	14	32	25
Risks surrounding the low interest rate environment	0	0	0	1	9	9
Risks around regulation/ taxes	1	1	3	3	3	8
Risk around property prices	3	1	3	1	3	7

SOURCE: Systemic Risk Survey 2013 H2, Bank of England
Units: % of respondents

Sovereign risk

Concerns about sovereign risk peaked at 94 per cent in the 2012 H2 survey and were focused around the possibility of default by eurozone member countries, although geopolitical risks related to Middle East instability (outside the top seven cited) were also at their highest. Likewise, sovereign risk, considered to have the greatest potential impact, also peaked at 68 per cent in the same survey.

Since then, sovereign risk concerns have abated to 74 per cent in Table 2.4.1 while remaining the most frequently cited. It was still considered to have the most severe potential impact at 39 per cent. While 65 per cent still highlight Europe as a particular region of concern in the 2013 H2 survey, 30 per cent also cited the possibility of US default, reflecting the uncertainty at that time of the likely outcome of negotiations on the US debt ceiling within Congress.

Risk of an economic downturn

Recognized as a risk of similar proportion to sovereign risk, fears of an economic downturn peaked at the beginning of 2011 (mentioned by 79 per cent) and remained at that level through to spring 2013 when it was rated as number one risk by 32 per cent. In the latest survey this risk was mentioned by 67 per cent and is still rated as the most serious by 25 per cent.

Given the more encouraging evidence of macro-economic recovery during January 2014 and, in the absence of bad news in the next few months, these risk ratings are likely to show further declines in the 2014 H1 survey.

Risks surrounding the low interest rate environment

The risk of a return to 'normal' interest rates was largely discounted up to the end of 2012. However, risk perceptions increased sharply during 2013 rising to 43 per cent rating in the 2013 H2 survey, but with only 9 per cent regarding this risk as one of the most significant, having risen from 1 per cent only in 2012 H2.

With the run-down in Bank of England tapering support during 2014, some increase in interest rates is now certain for 2015, if not on the 2014 horizon. The Bank of England Governor has backed down from the criterion of 7 per cent unemployment as the trigger for interest rate rises and has offered assurances that increments will be modest over a period. It will be interesting to see how sentiment is affected among the financial community in 2014 H1 survey findings.

In the 2014 H2 survey risks related to low interest rates were not exclusively associated with the effects of a sharp increase in interest rates (referred to by 40 per cent of respondents) but also risks arising from a long period of low rates such as the dampening effect of negative real interest rates on investment behaviour.

Risks around regulation or taxes

The perception of risks around the possible imposition of regulations and taxes also remain high with identification as a key risk by around 40 per cent of respondents.

The fears appear to be mainly about the impact of excessive, inconsistent or overly complex regulation of the financial sector rather than increases in taxation and, in any case, this category of risk is regarded as the most significant by only 8 per cent. With the certainty of a general election in May 2015, the likelihood of tax increases as opposed to taxpayer giveaways would appear to be remote.

Risks around property prices

Risks around property prices, almost exclusively in relation to a residential property bubble, have been perceived as a growing threat since the end of 2011 with 36 per cent of respondents listing them among their top five risks, an increase of 11 per cent since the 2013 H1 survey six months earlier. However, only 7 per cent of 2013 H2 respondents (3 per cent in 2013 H1) identify this as their paramount risk, probably because it is recognized that the Treasury and the Bank of England have a number of tools that they can deploy other than an interest rate rise to dampen demand (eg an increase in minimum deposit ratios for homeowner mortgages).

Other identified risks

Only two other categories of risk attracted 25 per cent or more of respondents' top five listings: risk of financial services failure/distress (30 per cent) and operational risk (25 per cent). Only 3 per cent highlighted the risk of financial failure/distress as their number one key risk, and operational risk was not regarded as a key risk by anyone.

In the first case, confidence that there will not be a failure/distress in financial services may be grounded on the evidence of continuing Treasury support for the vagaries of the two retail banks, RSB and Lloyds TSB, in part-public ownership. In the second case, the denial of acute operational risk in the financial services sector reflects a confidence in systems belied by the recent incidents of ATM and internet services failures.

Among the risks nominated by less than 20 per cent of respondents and high-lighted by none as number one are: risks surrounding monetary and fiscal policy; inflation risk; risk of tightening in credit conditions; and risks around anger against, or distrust of, financial institutions. Of these four, the first three are clearly low risk, at least for the short term in light of reassuring economic news and statements from the Bank of England Governor. The fourth, relating to public dislike and distrust of bankers and banking institutions, is more debatable. That the financial community considers risk from this source as inconsequential may be taken as a sign either of denial or indifference to the odium which bankers' pay attracts and poor customer relations. Essentially, any indifference is justified by the reality that businesses and individuals all have to live with the current banking services or in-surance premiums on offer and that dissatisfaction is likely to diminish as the 'feel good' factor revives.

Risks most challenging to manage as a firm

Respondents indicated the seven categories of risk that they would find the most difficult to manage in the following proportions (see Table 2.4.3).

TABLE 2.4.3   Most difficult risks to manage

	% of respondents
Sovereign risk	56
Risk of an economic downturn	33
Risks around regulation/taxes	29
Risks surrounding the low interest rate environment	23
Operational risk	16
Risk of financial market disruption/dislocation	14
Risk of financial institution failure/distress	14

SOURCE: Systemic Risk Survey 2013 H2, Bank of England

There is some correlation here between these findings and the previous identification of key risks to the UK financial system: the first two categories are cited in the same order. However, risks around regulation/taxes are considered rather harder to manage than risks surrounding the low interest rate environment whereas they were cited in reverse order in the key risks listing. Similarly, risk of financial institution failure/distress was listed two places ahead of risk of financial market disruption/dislocation and was awarded the same rating as a management challenge. Operational risk, rated as the number seven key risk, is considered more difficult to manage than either. Interestingly, risk around property prices which featured as the number five key risk is rated number eight among the most challenging risks.

Conclusion

The attitudes to key risks to the stability of the financial system by financial sector insiders are illuminating and their ratings may differ from those of other economic sectors. However, it is likely that manufacturing industry and other service sectors, if surveyed in the same way, would agree that the three most serious and challenging risks to their businesses are sovereign risk, risks of an economic downturn and of the low interest environment (or rather a major uplift of interest rates).

Above all, the underlying high levels of confidence that the financial services sector signals through these survey findings are encouraging. Like it or not, the sector is the bedrock of the modern UK economy and the other sectors cannot thrive when the financial sector falters.

PART THREE
Operational risk and key employment issues

Does your management system provide competitive advantage?

LRQA's technical expertise and sector specific experience ensures that our work is all about your business.

We work with over 5,000 organizations of all sizes across the global food supply chain. We offer assessment, certification and training services for all of the global food safety standards and schemes.

Further, we conduct second party and customized audits for many of the world's leading food companies and are at the forefront of the GFSI's Global Markets Programme.

For more information visit
www.food.lrqa.com

"LRQA's food assessors understand ACP and our supply chain and add real value to our business."

Stefan Speelmans
HSE & Quality Manager
ACP Europe

Lloyd's Register
LRQA

Improving performance, reducing risk

Getting food safety assessment right

COR GROENVELD, LRQA

"Harmonized standards, expert auditors and a consistent assessment methodology are working together to change the way food companies are managing risks.

Introduction

Contrary to the impression with which high-profile media coverage of food safety issues leaves us, the food that consumers eat today is at one of its safest points in its history. That is an incredible fact, when one takes into account the complexities in what is truly a 'global' food supply chain, with raw materials being grown on one continent, processed on another, packaged on yet another and then shipped and sold all over the world. The ability of large multinational food organizations to successfully manage the globalization of the food supply chain while minimizing the risks can largely be traced back to two key developments: firstly, the harmonization of global food safety standards and schemes, which has been driven by global retailers, manufacturers and their suppliers; and secondly, improvements in assessment methodologies and auditor competencies and calibration.

Harmonization of standards

As the food supply chain drastically expanded in the 1990s, it became clear to large organizations that it was not sufficient to know their direct suppliers. To successfully manage food safety, they needed to understand and manage the risks at every point in their supply chain. How to do that back then was not at all clear, with most large companies having their own food safety systems and processes, with little or no learnings from others. Food safety scares at this time led an influential group of retailers, manufacturers and certification bodies to join forces in an attempt to harmonize standards, increase transparency across the supply chain and share best practice. It was this key stakeholder understanding that food safety is non-competitive which led to a shift in philosophy towards sharing of systems, know-ledge and processes. In 2000, these organizations got together as the Global Food Safety Initiative (GFSI), with about 100 delegates attending their first global conference in Geneva. Today, organizations such as Walmart, Metro, Cargill, Danone, LRQA, DNV, Diversey Sealed Air, Trace One and Coca-Cola are but a few of the global, regional and local companies that are GFSI members and made up some of the 1,000-plus delegates that attended this year's 2014 GFSI Global Food Safety Conference in the United States.

Through their technical working groups, the GFSI has been instrumental in reducing what was previously hundreds of regional, industry and even company-specific standards and schemes to a manageable set of 12 GFSI-approved standards and schemes. The global leaders of the GFSI are now going through the process of educating, encouraging and mandating the certification of their suppliers to the same criteria. For most of the world, this has driven continual improvement, helped mitigate risks, led to increased efficiencies across the supply chain and helped suppliers reduce costs. Evidence of these improvements is now being shared by retailers like Metro and Walmart and manufacturers like Danone and Cargill at the GFSI conferences. Their data includes figures on the reduction of consumer complaints, recalls and wasted products.

The GFSI and its members have recognized that a successful food safety culture cannot be forced through the supply chain by the large multinationals alone. They have therefore also worked on a bottom-up approach, targeted at small suppliers and less developed countries. The GFSI's Global Markets Programme gives those suppliers a two-year window to gain an understanding of and implement one of the GFSI-approved standards and schemes. During those two years, the large global organizations, working together with a certification or training services provider, engage with the smaller suppliers to help them successfully implement a GFSI-approved scheme, and more importantly, the food safety culture that supports it.

Better auditors, better assessments

A firm commitment to a common set of standards, systems and processes allowed the food supply chain to benchmark and compare the manner in which organizations manage their risks. This began the shift in focus towards the auditors conducting the assessments and the methodologies that were being applied. LRQA, as one of the assessment bodies at the forefront of the GFSI movement, was an early supporter of the changes.

The auditor

Only through assessors with sector-specific expertise and relevant experience in the food industry could the assessment and certification process truly add value to the global food supply chain. As more organizations began to understand the benefits of third-party certification, the demand for it increased substantially. In order to meet that demand, certification bodies needed more and more auditors. For some, that meant a reduction in the qualifications and training of auditors. That fact was highlighted at the 2011 GFSI conference, where auditor competency was listed as the number one concern for food safety professionals. The integrity of the assessments and the certificate are of the utmost importance and can only demonstrate their true value when delivered by a trained auditor who possesses assessment skills but who also has sufficient sector knowledge.

The second thing that is really important is that an auditor has to ensure that he or she really looks in depth at the corporate objectives and strategies and understands the vision of the company. From there, the auditor needs to find out what are the real risks in the organization and the processes and focus on these risks. It has to be a risk-based approach, which is the only way that an auditor can do an effective audit. Essentially effective auditors need to be bilingual – they need to be able to speak the language of the shop floor as well as that of the boardroom to achieve a complete understanding of an organization.

Thirdly, the certification process has to be linked to driving improvement. Again, the technical expertise of the auditor and the certification process has to support the company to drive continuous improvement. An auditor can challenge the organization, without being a consultant of course, and support the organization by doing a robust and in-depth assessment. And of course, when any deviations with a stated requirement against the standard of risks for food safety are found, the auditor needs to raise a finding of non-conformity. Depending on the risk, it will be graded as a minor or major, or with other similar grading terminology. The ability to raise these findings and avoid 'soft grading' is also critical in an audit. It is not acceptable to have differences – even if there are sometimes cultural influences. To look at this positively, a finding of non-conformity is also an opportunity to improve.

Finally, the calibration of auditors has to ensure the same level of assessment across international boundaries. Calibration assures global organizations that their assessments have been delivered in the same, robust way, the reports are detailed and consistent, and that their operations are effective and conforming to the relevant standard or scheme. Organizations like Cargill are taking a global, integrated approach to supply chain and food safety. Mark Overland, Director for Global Certification at Cargill, said: 'We're rolling out FSSC 22000 (a GFSI-recognized food safety management certification scheme, based on ISO 22000) to over 1,000 plants in 67 different countries. Having the same level of food safety execution at every plant is an expectation from our customers.'

The assessment

As the GFSI and its members were focusing on the shortage of high-quality food auditors, a change was also taking place in the way that assessments were conducted. The industry had largely followed the 'snapshot in time' approach, whereby the company being assessed prepared for the visit and simply made sure that 'everything was right on that day'. Provided all was in order and the list could be checked off, then a certificate was issued.

A more effective, process-based management systems approach was being delivered by the more skilled auditors and certification bodies, but not yet formalized through the standards and schemes against which they were assessing. This led to a wide variance in the way that assessments were being carried out, even within the same client and same certification body. The introduction in 2004 of ISO 22000, the first global food safety management system standard, began a slow change in approach, with the launch in 2008 of the FSSC 22000 certification scheme (which incorporated sector-specific food safety prerequisite programme requirements) being the 'marker in the sand' needed for the food industry to make its move to the process- and system-based approach. FSSC 22000 has been the engine for a process- and system-audit approach in the food supply chain. No longer is it how the factory looks on Tuesday at 11am that determines if a food safety certificate hangs on the wall. Now it is an in-depth look at the underpinning systems and processes by a qualified, calibrated auditor that is helping organizations of all sizes manage their food safety risks.

Assessment as a valuable tool

A thorough and probing assessment and certification process can only be delivered when auditors with in-depth knowledge and sector-specific expertise assess against a robust process and systems-based assessment methodology.

ACP Europe, a specialist in the provision of carbon dioxide and a longtime LRQA client, is a strong example of an organization leading the way in the new world of food safety. Combining the GFSI approach through their consistent adoption of FSSC 22000 whilst focusing on the value that qualified, sector-specific assessors can bring to their organization, ACP has embedded a risk-based food safety culture. 'FSSC 22000 delivers a whole new approach to risk management and quality assurance,' explains Stefan Speelmans, ACP Europe Safety Health Environmental Quality Manager. 'Through LRQA's approach, our whole network of interacting processes is assessed and monitored, thus providing greater assurance to both internal and external stakeholders and protecting our brand reputation.'

The implementation of FSSC 22000 has also proven to lead to significant financial savings. The cost savings in real terms are potentially huge and the value of harmonization is clearly supported by Wrigley, a subsidiary of Mars, Incorporated, who stated that: 'Wrigley's North American factories saw on average a 25–50 per cent reduction of audits by retailers with the adoption of FSSC 22000'.

Conclusion

At LRQA, we believe that a robust assessment approach, one that looks at an organization's integrated management system and processes, embeds continual improvement as a fundamental component and features a risk-based methodology, certainly helps to mitigate risks and drive food safety and sustainability across the global food supply chain.

LRQA has worked proactively with food supply chain stakeholders, including manufacturers, retailers, suppliers and industry experts to move the food sector away from a checklist-based approach to auditing towards a process-based management systems approach. This approach looks at the underlying systems and processes that organizations have in place rather than the ability of that plant or factory to convince an auditor on a given day that they comply with a series of items on a checklist. It is not enough to have a strong standard or scheme; organizations need registrars or certification bodies that:

- offer auditors who have extensive experience and proven competence in the sectors they are auditing;
- can provide a robust process-based management systems approach to assessment;
- are prepared to stand up to the client when non-conformities are found; and finally
- help the organizations being assessed to reduce risks, improve food safety performance and link their food safety management systems objectives to their overall corporate objectives.

What is clear is that organizations across the food supply chain, including some of the world's leading manufacturers and retailers, are increasingly recognizing the benefits of independent assessment and certification, not only in terms of the cost savings, but also in terms of the benefits and value it brings.

Those organizations that are prioritizing potential auditor CVs and certification body methodologies and credentials, rather than focusing on price, have clearly understood what is at stake. This approach is helping to drive consumer and other key stakeholder confidence as well as ultimately helping to safeguard the lives of people around the world. On the road to food safety, this can only be seen as a positive step.

Follow us on Twitter @LRQA or visit **www.lrqa.com**

The role of risk management in enhancing performance

ALLAN GIFFORD

Introduction

Delegates at the 2014 World Economic Forum in Davos were told that good mental and physical health is one of the most pressing social and economic issues of the day. It may seem obvious that a healthier population makes for a happier society and a more productive economy. So with national economies struggling, stabilizing, and some recovering, risk management has a role to play in ensuring the health of organizations; ensuring that whether they be private or public sector, charitable or profit-making, large or small, new or old, they achieve what they have set out to do.

Of course what they each seek to do is different and therefore risk management itself has differing roles to play in their performance. For some, success will be in protection – protection of revenue, life, property, the environment, or the brand. For others, out of adversity comes opportunity and for some organizations the perils of austerity, climate change or national crises bring potential to exploit new-found situations, thus creating wealth or shareholder value – an outcome that must appear against the odds. Regulated organizations will find that challenging times often come hand-in-hand with yet more regulation. For them, success is about good governance, compliance, and avoiding fines, unwelcome surprises and negative attention. Some might attempt to ride the storm and remain intact for when they come out of the other side. To be successful then requires the retention of talent and intellectual capital which will ultimately contribute to what will be a competitive position once the big spenders start to feel more confident again.

Whichever type of organization, they all have something in common. They have stated a purpose, probably articulated through success measures and strategies in place to achieve it all. They also, therefore, have set out the performance they require from their people, partners and other stakeholders. They also, though, have invited ambiguity, uncertainty and vulnerability in decision making and behaviours.

Is risk management up to the job?

As risk management professionals we talk about the many reasons why organizations undertake risk management. We often justify risk management activity in terms of reductions of accidents or injury, savings in insurance premiums, or compliance with codes of practice. We play at all levels in an organization: in the boardroom, in management committees and on the shop floor. We engage externally as well as internally, seeking to influence rating agencies, owners, lenders, insurers, our staff and suppliers, also our local communities.

But what do we do to help our organizations understand the direct line of sight from day-to-day decisions and tasks to organizational success? How can we advise and demonstrate to our organizations that breaking down the high-level objectives into individual activities and tasks enables the description of the performance required of all the operating units? By default, the collective achievement of the myriad of these activities and tasks should result in the achievement of our organizational success. In between these two ends of the spectrum are all those things that can go right or wrong and help or hinder their achievement. In other words, the risk management.

So risk management must provide active, no – proactive – advice and support to organization leaders. It must be an efficient machinery of live, accurate and always current information on which leaders can make decisions. Risk management must be fit for its purpose which in terms of performance management means that it must be attached to all the parts of the organization, be they strategic in nature, financial, operational or regulatory. This fitness for purpose means that the risk management arrangements must reflect the current organization and its internal and external context.

Risk management must provide the advice, tools, products and services that assist an organization with its planning and reporting, feeding into and influencing decisions surrounding resources, priorities and, increasingly, helping to manage expectations. And just in case of things not going according to plan, risk management provides arrangements through business continuity management to minimize damage, deal with crises and recover back to normality, perhaps even reach a better place.

Risk management helps overcome performance management challenges

So what challenges do organizations face when monitoring and managing their performance? Leadership teams are accountable for their organization's success and put in place mechanisms by which to measure progress towards it. Risk management has a role to play in these mechanisms.

One feature of performance management is reporting. It's not uncommon to hear people bemoan how much reporting takes place these days. We all understand that what gets measured gets done, but quite often we can't see the wood for the trees.

To maintain focus on doing the right things organizations need to link their tasks and activities with strategic objectives and organizational success. This must happen at all levels of the organization: from boardroom, through region or division, right to the coal face. Each component of an organization plays its own part in the overall success and for performance to be managed it is important to make sure that the constituent parts have a direct line of sight to organizational success (see Figure 3.2.1).

FIGURE 3.2.1   Direct line of sight between activities/tasks and organizational success

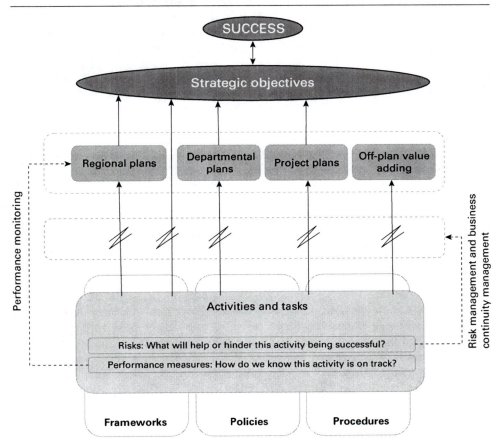

Risk management exists at all levels in an organization and therefore is directly connected to the achievement of organizational success. This chapter describes a few examples of how this happens.

Five common challenges

The first challenge that leaders face is that some key drivers of success are not easily measured. Organizations usually express success through hard measures. But behaviour or attitudes have a significant contribution. People are often cited as the organization's greatest asset but we don't always see behavioural traits expressed in performance management reporting.

Of course it's difficult to put a measure on flexibility, innovation, how knowledge and intellectual property is actually used, and so on. But these are important human aspects. They close deals, retain loyal customers, identify efficiencies, save money, have people working late to ensure that deliveries take place, and so on. Risk management helps by articulating the skills and competencies that are required for people to manage the risks inherent in their work, and providing suitable training.

That said – and perhaps therefore – challenge number 2 is that behaviour is not always in line with strategic objectives. If the wrong things are measured then either the wrong things will be done, or opportunities will be missed. For so long employees have been working in fear and survival mode, doing their job in such a way as to make sure they don't lose it. Therefore irrelevant measures go unchallenged, and even if the performance is excellent, if it's not the required performance then less than optimum outcomes arise, along with resentment and resistance. Through risk-based assurance mapping an organization can ensure that the right things are being done, in the right way, by the right people.

Thirdly, the performance management system can sometimes conflict with the culture of the organization. The type of organization is an important consideration when designing and implementing a method of managing performance. There's no point having an overly bureaucratic system for a highly entrepreneurial company. What is actually getting rewarded … 'political skills' or operating performance?

Reward and recognition must be aligned for performance management to have motivational impact as well as provide management information for decision making. Risk management helps by clarifying ownership and accountability for risks or controls. This puts definite boundaries around where responsibilities start and stop, ensuring that risk-related leadership, education and involvement occurs.

Challenge number 4 is that the development of measures can be time-consuming or difficult. It's fair to say that not all activities of an organization have the direct line of sight to strategic objectives. Some activities are clearly value-adding, but not directly derived from an objective. So it's not only the direction of the organization's travel that needs measurement, but other things too. Creating many measures can take a great deal of time and management attention, the effort itself often being questioned for its efficacy. Effective risk management looks at the interconnectivity of risks and considers the characteristics of possible causes, and the variety of possible consequences of events. Linking this depth of risk analysis to organizational activities enables the measures of general 'good things to do' to have purpose.

Last but by no means least, continual change makes effective planning essential. This requires review and refinement. Change is one of the givens in today's operating environment, and just like the monitoring and review of any risk management framework, a performance management system should be regularly assessed for its fitness for purpose. The quality world preaches the 'plan–do–check–act' cycle which we know makes perfect sense. Yet still we know (but still do little about it) that organizations are better at the 'plan' and 'do', not bad at the 'check', but generally and consistently fall short in the 'act'. A performance management system that doesn't adjust itself for organizational changes, whether they are internal operations or an updated strategy, will have less use. A good risk management framework will refresh itself against constant change through regular internal and often external, independent, reviews. It should be easy to align the performance management system to these reviews. Aligning risk management itself to a recognized framework such as ISO 31000 will help with this.

Trends in performance management

Despite the challenges inherent in performance management, risk managers are responding in a number of ways. As a result, today's professional risk managers are better expressing the value that risk management offers to organizations, making a direct and demonstrable benefit to bottom line, and are raising their profiles in boardrooms.

The emergence and increase of key risk indicators (KRIs) is helping to link performance management and risk management. Fuelled by the interest in risk appetite in recent years, KRIs, although having been around for some time, have attracted the attention of senior managers as a way of linking risk-related activity to the achievement of organizational objectives. KRIs talk in a language and structure that leaders can relate to. They can describe quantitative information but also behaviour and people's actions.

Risk management's impact on performance management is that uncertain, uncontrollable events can be better understood and planned for, helping the organization to better join up risk management and business continuity management (a connection that still not everyone is able to grasp).

Increasingly, today's risk managers are competent in strategy and planning. Risk managers have heard the wishes of their organizations to become more business savvy and are undertaking the required learning, whether personally or professionally, in 'managing business'. The route of risk manager being promoted from insurance buyer is gradually being replaced by the recruitment of MBAs or professionals from other business disciplines. Corporate risk teams are being structured and resourced according to the skills and competencies required by the organizations, rather than by promoting or transferring in from, for example, health and safety or claims management.

Therefore, whereas organizations often still operate in silos, risk management departments understand that they need to be cross-functional. The impact on performance management is better aggregation of risk information, giving improved input into horizon scanning, resulting in improved organizational foresight.

In such austere times as we have at the moment, organizations are accepting that 'hitting target' might indeed be difficult and therefore what is important is at least to 'do better'. Either do better than the competition, better than this time last year, better than the industry benchmark – whatever. But basically to do better, compared with something else. As a result, organizations are allowing comparative as well as fixed performance measures. For the time being, it might be enough for organizational survival to do better than someone or something else.

This philosophy maintains operational focus in the tough times as well as the good. Risk management is similarly about the tough times as well as the good, and mechanisms for articulating upside as well as downside risk help organizations to express 'what success looks like'.

Performance is the responsibility of all managers. But, it can manifest itself as an administrative task (reporting, performance appraisals) rather than an embedded discipline. Performance management should align targets and measures, which are delivered through tasks, actions and behaviours.

We often hear about performance management being led by Human Resources which, through tools such as balanced scorecards and individual targets, is a quite acceptable approach. But it's more than this. Performance management is also part of change management, operations management, financial management and so on, and of course risk management too. A variety of internal 'systems' track performance across an organization. By having oversight of the entire organization's activities and plans the risk management function is starting to lead, coordinate and govern organizations' performance management.

Driven by worries over measuring too much, leadership teams are initiating reviews of performance management frameworks and are looking to their risk management departments to make improvement recommendations. Risk management functions are ideally placed to do this because they contain both qualitative skills of strategists and process people, and quantitative talent that can turn data into insight. Risk management departments have frameworks that inherently attend to a wide variety of organizational matters such as quality, flexibility, compliance, strategy, stakeholders; deal externally and internally; and take the varying perspectives of here and now, the next three years and also the longer-term sustainability.

This topic of sustainability is also where the risk management function is contributing more to organizations. The previous obsession with pure financial performance is decreasing as organizations better understand the trade-off between hitting financial results and delivering a sustainable organization socially and environmentally.

Using risk management techniques, organizations increasingly understand the material risks from the perspective of their internal and external stakeholders. This can surface differing priorities for performance reporting. It also highlights specific needs for resources, capabilities and competencies, and might identify internal process improvements.

The concept of multiple stakeholders will also influence the multiple dimensions that performance management frameworks need to have, and the link performance reporting has to good corporate governance.

Summary

So risk management sits at both ends of the planning and performance management continuum. It inputs into and informs strategic planning but also takes the output of strategic decision making for the purposes of understanding what can help or hinder the successful achievement of objectives.

Risk management has both soft and technical skills. This is coming about through investment in training and development, both by individuals and provided by employers. Today's risk managers have an organization-wide perspective and are increasingly being seen as business advisers: the internal business consultant. As a result, the role of risk management in performance management is elevated from administrator to driver.

Finally, risk management helps all the activities of an organization by connecting tasks to overall strategic success. In some cases that is through a direct line of sight, in other cases it is about connecting all 'the various things that go on' in order to understand and present the complexity of an organization and interdependencies of silo tasks.

Managing risks in the supply chain: reaching new standards

STEVE CULP, ACCENTURE FINANCE & RISK SERVICES

Introduction

Preventing supply chain interruptions is undoubtedly one of the central purposes of supply chain management; indeed, most supply chain managers would say that they spend too much of their time managing risk issues, ranging from delivery delays to product quality issues. While traditional supply chain risk management has allowed corporations to deal with the most well-known supply chain concerns, recent events have shown that more specific and more sophisticated risk management methods are essential to better protect globalized supply chains.

Recent events – including Typhoon Haiyan hitting the Philippines, the 2011 Japanese earthquake and tsunami, the floods in Thailand and the ash clouds caused by the 2010 Icelandic volcano eruption – have demonstrated how far the consequences of such risks can extend. The incurred losses were a warning to C-level executives across the globe about how exposed their supply chains can be. The Japanese earthquake severely affected global electronics production and led to extended business disruptions for the automotive industry. The Thai flooding created significant shortages in the hard disk drive market that generated hundreds of millions of dollars of losses for well-known electronics manufacturers.

Aside from these headline events, however, the nature of supply chain risks is constantly changing. New risks and new vulnerabilities require close attention from management. Counterfeited products, for example, have entered supply chains in greater numbers and can inflict lasting damage on a company's perceived product quality and reputation. Original equipment manufacturers seeking to ensure the continuity of their operations have increasing concerns about supplier solvency at times of high volatility in financial markets or currencies. The financial crisis that emerged in 2008 has shown how reduced access to credit can have an impact on the less financially stable companies and create headaches for supply chain managers.

Current supply chain fragilities are not just related to emerging risks; they are as much a result of supply and network design strategies as they are driven by a limited integration of risk management into supply chain management.

In light of these and other concerns, companies recognize the need for a more formal management of supply chain risks. They need to rethink their operative model to define an optimum balance between financial efficiency and control over the supply chain.

Current business models are more vulnerable to supply chain risks

The continuing focus on operational efficiency and cost optimization has been a strategic priority over the last few decades, helping corporations lower the cost of manufacturing through outsourcing, offshoring and other practices. Cost reduction efforts, however, often outweighed other strategic priorities. Companies that once kept back-up inventory and manufacturing facilities in place may have exposed themselves to additional risk as they concentrated on working with fewer redundancies.

New supply chain models generate new risks

The Kaizen model has become the basis for the lean strategies that have become so popular globally. Key components of this model include just-in-time or even just-in-sequence production, with minimal in-process inventories, geographic and operational concentration of assembly and parts production, and a high level of subcontracting. While lean management has provided significant advantages in terms of cost reduction and increased manufacturing efficiency, it also increases risk velocity and impact.

For many companies, make-or-buy decisions have been decided in favour of buying, not making. While this reduces manufacturing overhead, companies lose oversight of key governance and management strategies and introduce unknown risks into the supply chain. Periodic risk rebalancing is essential.

Globalization of supply chains as a risk factor

Many companies switched from local suppliers to low-cost and often distant suppliers on the basis of cost optimization, without considering the cost of risks caused by this strategic change. Larger companies now buy from smaller suppliers in very remote areas of the globe. The extended supply chain now has many additional points of potential failure, requiring new approaches to risk management. Companies face longer logistics lead times, as well as new and unfamiliar risk profiles encompassing natural disasters, epidemics, and social, political or monetary instability.

A global supply chain also increases risks related to supply chain integrity, compliance and quality control. Relationships with remote partners are subject to differences in business and cultural practices. Such risks are difficult to forecast and monitor, creating gaps in the risk management capability for most companies. Realizing the systemic nature of supply chain risks, some companies are reviewing their purchasing strategies and practices, and rethinking the way they are doing business.

Because risk is a key factor of financial performance, the absence of qualitative and quantitative valuation can affect overall desired business outcomes. Improving the understanding, valuation and management of those systemic risks will provide a clear contribution to decreasing the cost of risks for each transaction.

The challenges with classical risk management and risk transfer strategies

Classic risk management methods have proved inefficient in addressing these new supply chain risks. Many companies are operating with insufficient insurance coverage of key risks. Insurers do not always understand rapidly evolving supply chain risks; it is easier, from an underwriting perspective, to insure a company's own facility than it is to insure against disruptions related to multi-tiered suppliers in multiple, far-flung locations.

In recent years, property and casualty insurers have significantly improved the scope of underwriting services to cover supply chain disruptions. They are now providing business interruption insurance for disruptions occurring at a supplier's facilities, although with coverage constraints that reduce the efficiency of risk transfer. Risk coverage is provided by most insurers for named suppliers or facilities only and does not cover the whole network of suppliers and subcontractors. Coverage limits are also usually low and not adequate to sufficiently insure against a larger part of the risk exposure, leaving a significant part of the risk uninsured. Partial coverage, as much as self-insurance, can prove costly, especially in the event of a loss. This makes the actual identification and management of supply chain risks even more important.

Another traditional challenge for risk management is related to the fact that risk managers are not typically in a position to influence strategic and operational business decisions; owing to the structural separation between a traditionally more risk-reporting-focused function and operational decision making, they are more often than not called in after the fact rather than during the planning process, while risk management requires more operational integration.

In fact, most companies do not have a risk function in the supply chain that would review risk appetite and risk tolerance through the supply chain to take action to address specific risks that the company could not bear. While traditional risk reporting – focused on collecting and prioritizing risk reports from operations to inform senior managers – is useful for corporate governance purposes, it is mostly inadequate to develop proactive risk management and prevention strategies.

While one might wonder why there is no further integration of risk management into operations, the low frequency of larger supply chain disruptions and the efficient management of experienced supply chain professionals are probably the most likely reasons. The natural tendency to assume that events that have not happened in the past are not likely to happen in the future should not prevent corporations from upgrading their risk management practices to meet new standards. Better practices undoubtedly contribute to helping corporations achieve their business goals.

Improving the management of risks in the supply chain

There are a number of effective approaches to dealing with new types and levels of supply chain risk. One of the most important principles for organizations to bear in mind is to start with increasing the visibility of inherent risks; it is impossible to plan for and difficult to manage risks that have not been envisioned. Unforeseen events of recent years have shown that limited risk scenario analysis and planning lead to gaps in the risk management framework.

Among the tools available for charting risk are:

- *Scenario planning.* Scenario planning is a key step in improving supply chain risk management. It examines the underlying factors affecting the supply chain, including political, logistical and technological dimensions, as well as global economic factors. As part of scenario planning, probability modelling can help identify unknown risks and develop contingency plans for business continuity.

- *Financial quantification and modelling.* These tools work on several levels, first as an operational decision-making tool (many software vendors have developed solutions specifically for supply chain modelling) and also as a strategic risk management tool.

- *Ongoing measurement of risks.* Close attention to changes in key performance indicators (KPIs) along with detailed risk reporting and monitoring can provide valuable insight and early warning of new conditions.

- *Improving the 'traceability' of the supply chain.* More and more organizations are following key deliverables through the entire supply chain and identifying risks not only among top-tier suppliers but among lower-tier suppliers and their subcontractors.

With a clearer understanding of the risks facing the organization – and the potential financial, operational and reputational consequences of those risks – it is much easier to address the question of how to integrate risk management into business operations and ensure its effectiveness. Key steps include:

1 *Look at the whole, not just the parts.* Companies tend to look at risk in individual parts such as procurement, logistics, distribution or manufacturing. Most risks, however, should be managed across the supply chain network. Because of the systemic nature of supply chain risks, a problem in one area can easily affect the entire supply chain and the entire organization. Such risks must be identified, managed and communicated throughout the network.

The assessment process may begin with a look at all suppliers, including third-party vendors and counterparties. The operational and financial risk profile of each vendor should be inventoried, and the vendor's own risk management processes should be identified.

Similarly, all risks can be measured by their impact, not only within their own function, but across the company and all the way to the customers. Measurements of risk should incorporate reputational and market share impacts that can have lasting effects on a corporation's business. In order to be able to aggregate risks, sophisticated supply chain management software is increasingly required in order to measure interdependencies within the entire value chain, and help quantify financially what are the most effective options to manage or mitigate risk.

2 *Review the governance of the organization's risks.* The risk function is too often focused on reporting risks that are well known within operating units, with less ability to ensure that the scope of risks under consideration is adequate and includes less frequent risks that could have a much higher impact. These risks encompass the entire supply chain and include business continuity, creditworthiness of suppliers, currency risk, commodity volatility, supply chain integrity, political risks and a number of other operational risks. A holistic approach to risk management with a clearer focus on identifying and preventing risks, rather than reporting, is essential to moving risk management from a risk response function to risk anticipation and prevention.

Ideally, the risk management structure and capability should match the company's risk appetite, and be sized to reflect how much risk the organization is willing to take. This implies a clear quantification of the risk appetite as well as operational vulnerabilities in order to define the adequate structure and depth of risk management. The company that strives for maximum efficiency should have highly efficient and integrated risk management to reflect this larger risk appetite.

3 *Review current operating models.* The adequate range and scope of risk management changes can only be achieved through an in-depth analysis of the risk embedded into a company's operating model, and through an additional review of all procedures and controls intended to manage those risks. Typical steps are a systematic review of the supply chain risk inventory, the identification of critical single points of failure in the organization, and the end-to-end quantification of the financial impact those key risks can generate. As painstaking as it seems, this process is key to defining how to improve risk management practices, systems and related governance.

Some companies are, for example, re-examining the benefits of global versus local processes to determine which operations should be centralized and which should be managed locally. A comprehensive procurement review may, in some cases, point the way toward bringing some suppliers back onshore or adjusting the risk management framework to concentrate on clearly identified risks, while considering key issues such as currency fluctuations or rising transport costs.

4 *Integrate risk management into operations planning and management, in terms of both functions and workflow.* Typically, the risk function is 'headquarters centred' and less likely to provide input into the daily decision-making process for operations, including procurement, manufacturing, supply chain and logistics. To change this, a risk management function that contributes to the strategic, sales and operational planning processes would factor in key risks in the decision-making process. This newly designed risk management function in the supply chain can contribute to improving the risk management capability in the current organizational set-up but can also ensure that the right amount of risk management flows into key supply chain decisions.

Leading car manufacturers are currently reviewing their operating model for risk purposes, aiming to increase the standardization of non-differentiated parts, together with an increase of multiple sourcing strategies. While there is a cost associated with these changes, most corporations will be able to achieve overall cost savings while reducing current and future risks in their supply chain.

5 *Use a financial modelling capability for the supply chain.* Because management of the supply chain is increasingly complex, using advanced supply chain modelling tools is essential for scenario planning as well as supply chain design and risk quantification. This capability can in particular achieve the following:

– Gauge the financial impact of supply volatility on supply chain economics.

– Analyse the impact of product and service demand volatility.

– Measure the impact that launching a new product or entering a new market can have on long-term production capacity.

– Quantify the cost of operational disruptions.

– Balance the distribution of risk between the company and its customer, suppliers and joint venture partners.

– Use financial products to mitigate procurement, manufacturing and distribution risks.

6 *Improve risk reporting and monitoring.* Risk management is benefiting from performance management systems that help monitor key performance indicators to identify problems and take corrective measures quickly. Dashboards and scoring models are increasingly becoming a risk manager's tool for areas such as supplier solvency or supplier quality management. Real-time risk monitoring capabilities used in combination with mapping software are also providing supply chain managers with techniques to track key supply chain flows from supplier locations to manufacturing facilities through to final customers. Such tools speed response in the case of numerous unplanned events, such as political conflict or natural catastrophes. Based upon our experience and research in the space, companies with the most dependent supply chains such as electronics or high-tech manufacturers have for the most part already integrated these tools into their standard supply chain management practices.

Taking risk management live

The increased understanding of how vulnerable supply chains are has strengthened the case for companies to enhance their risk management practices and systems. Most corporations have also realized that the cost of effective risk management is significantly lower than the cost of dealing with supply chain disruptions. Proactive prevention measures pay for themselves many times over. In the context of heightened pressures on operating costs and the need to improve business efficiency permanently, the risk function will play a key role in identifying the best opportunities to rebalance operational efficiency with risk management. This is a key step in avoiding unnecessary vulnerability in the operating model.

The trend is clear. Leading manufacturers that previously focused almost solely on efficiency as the primary metric of success are now actively changing their supply chain business models to incorporate risk-based and cost-effective supply chain management to balance the overall definition of success. Companies need to consider reviewing their own business models and identify how best to raise their capability for managing supply chain risks. This can, at times of great uncertainty and volatility, prove to be a key differentiator and a source of competitive advantage.

The importance of managing health and safety and environmental risk

RON REID, SHOOSMITHS LLP

Judith Hackitt, the Chair of the Health and Safety Executive (HSE), the UK's national independent regulator for work-related safety and health, said in a speech in London in December 2013 that she was concerned when any organization stated that health and safety was their number one priority. Her view was that it ought not to be the case, as most organizations, other than perhaps those providing health and safety services, are not in business for that purpose. Their main focus usually lies elsewhere, be it the manufacturing of goods or the provision of services and all need to be profitable at it. Therefore, in order to successfully manage health and safety and environmental risk in any organization, the controlling of such risks should become a core value, built into the very fabric of that organization.

Basic risk management

In theory, at least, the management of risk in these areas should be simple. Once all has been done to design out risks at source, the residual risk properly assessed and then policies and procedures put in place to minimize each of those risks, compliance should follow. When done well, safe working procedures will minimize both safety and environmental risks. The challenge for management is to ensure that they are well communicated and understood and that people are trained to be competent in performing their work-related task in accordance with safe working practice. Once an organization has reached this stage then they are left with what is often the most difficult part, namely, behavioural safety.

Getting people within organizations to perform their tasks in a habitually safe way that follows best practice can be difficult; often calling for behavioural safety programmes to improve the safety culture within an organization. It has to be appreciated, however, that there is no such thing as zero risk, only the lowest possible residual risk.

How to improve risk management

Good health and safety and environmental management will only be achieved within an organization by installing safe behaviours as a core value. That requires careful planning, delivery, action and audit. However, above all these is the need for good leadership. This needs to start from the very top and continue throughout the line management chain with good behaviours being enforced and reinforced constantly so that they are seen as a core value by those working within the organization, as well as by those affected by its activities. Defining good leadership can be difficult in itself: it has been said that being a true leader is not about rank and that a person is only really a leader when people follow them. But what is certainly the case is that the lowest standard exhibited by the leaders of an organization is the highest standard that that organization can expect of those working for it.

Importance of culture

Installing health, safety and environmental compliance as a core value is intrinsically intertwined with the wider culture of an organization. Only by good communication and consultation with employees are you likely to arrive at working practices which are accepted and fully understood by those who are expected to implement them. Getting buy-in at an early stage will help gain acceptance of them as practical working methods.

For many organizations, managing health and safety and environmental risk is a corporate governance issue, as well as an integral part of their corporate social responsibility. Serious failures in this area can and do adversely affect the stability of, or perhaps even the continuance of, organizations themselves.

The culture of an organization will come under intense scrutiny should there be a failing in environmental or health and safety performance which leads to a serious incident or accident.

A fatal accident at work, for example, will immediately lead to investigation of any failings on the part of organizations having a duty of care towards the deceased and of individuals within it. The possibility of prosecution for corporate manslaughter is a primary consideration for those investigating such accidents. As the evidence required to prove corporate manslaughter is that an organization, by the way in which its affairs have been managed or organized, has fallen far below the standard expected of it, then it can be seen that culture is crucial.

In such investigations, the roles of each of the individuals throughout the line management chain are scrutinized, the aim being to determine whether they were failures of senior management and whether unsafe practices were both commonplace and tolerated. This can lead to personal criminal liability for senior management as well as the prosecution of the organization. Personal liability can take the form of a prosecution for gross negligence and manslaughter since 2003 in the UK; all such convictions have resulted in immediate terms of imprisonment being imposed.

Enforcement trends

Since the introduction of the UK corporate manslaughter legislation, the police lead all investigations into fatal accidents, with technical support from the Health & Safety Executive (HSE). In the past they would often hand the investigation over to the HSE at an early stage. This is no longer the case.

The HSE itself has changed its policy in recent years. Since 2008 their enforcement policy has required them, when investigating an incident, to consider the roles played by individuals throughout the line management chain and to prosecute them where appropriate, either alongside or instead of the organizations for which they work.

The statistics in relation to personal prosecution reflect this trend. As at the end of 2013, 89 persons had received sentences of imprisonment for offences under health and safety legislation since it was first introduced on 1st January 1975. Importantly, however, of that number, 78 have received such a sentence since 2008. This trend is set to continue. In practice, it leads to conflicts of interest between those individuals and the organization requiring separate legal advice and representation and considerable additional cost.

Other regulators are following suit with fire authorities leading the way. Individual prosecutions for breach of environmental regulation are not unknown alongside the well-known general proposition that the polluter must pay.

Regulators often share their findings amongst one another. This sharing of 'intelligence' can come from some obvious and, sometimes, less than obvious sources such as adverse insurance company audits.

In high-risk industries, the Environment Agency and the HSE are charged to work closely together as the 'competent authority' overseeing business where a failing may give rise to a major hazard or accident. However increasingly, actual harm to either persons or the environment is not a prerequisite for enforcement action by the authorities.

No need for actual harm

Recent years have seen an increasing trend towards enforcement action being taken for the potential for harm being caused, rather than actual harm having to be proved. Simply failing to prevent risk to others is sufficient for liability to arise. In the UK, once the relevant enforcing authority has shown that a duty-holder's actions have given rise to a risk, then the burden of proving that they have done all that is reasonably practical to prevent that risk passes to the duty-holder if they are to successfully defend themselves. In effect, unlike most criminal sanctions the defendant must prove themselves innocent.

CASE STUDY   The Sellafield case study

Sellafield Ltd processes and stores nuclear waste. In January 2014, it appealed to the UK Court of Appeal seeking to have a total fine of £700,000 reduced.

The company had pleaded guilty to environmental and safety offences arising from failing to correctly dispose of four bags of very low level radioactive waste. It had been identified as fit for disposal to a landfill site and was part of 5,000 bags that were correctly identified. Three of the bags reached the landfill site and were handled by workers there. However, the level of radiation they were exposed to was less than a passenger would receive on a flight from London to Paris.

It was accepted by the court that no actual harm had been caused to those exposed.

The court focused on the management failures which had been found not to be confined to certain individuals or management levels, but rather demonstrated 'a custom within the company which was too lax and... to a degree complacent for which senior management must bear its share of responsibility'.

The court disallowed the appeal stating that the level of fine had achieved its statutory purpose by bringing home to the directors and shareholders the seriousness of offences committed.

Courts in future will look closely at both the turnover and profit of defendants before deciding the level of fine that will achieve this outcome.

How can you determine and improve your current risk culture?

In order to assess your current culture and perhaps to avoid complacency, a number of steps can be taken:

- bring together small groups of line managers and workers to get a true picture of behaviours;
- identify those tasks and activities with behaviours that put people or the environment at risk;
- find ways of measuring those behaviours that are safety critical;

- recruit and train observers in the workplace to challenge, feed back and review behaviours that are outside agreed baselines;
- keep management and workers involved by giving constructive feedback on undesirable behaviours whilst remembering to praise those that are desirable.

Once you have gathered the findings, use them to set challenging but realistic targets to improve performance. Many organizations which have personal appraisal systems in place set such targets at all levels, often with considerable success.

Conclusion

The risk to any business of poor environmental and health and safety risk management is considerable. The UK courts are imposing ever-increasing levels of fine and sending a clear message to all organizations that one of their overriding objectives should be to achieve a safe environment. Failure to do that will result in them imposing fines large enough to underline that message not only to those who manage the organization but to their shareholders.

Going forward, businesses failing to properly control these risks could easily face penalties that they are unlikely to survive.

Those successful at managing these risks have strong leadership and compliance as a core value. Good intentions are not sufficient. Many high-profile safety cases over the years have been routed in the failure of leadership. As was said in the report following the public inquiry into the Clapham Junction rail accident as long ago as 1988: 'A concern for safety which is sincerely held and repeatedly expressed but nevertheless is not carried through into action is as much protection from danger as no concern at all'.

Women on boards: the UK Corporate Governance Code requirements and the Irish experience

SINEAD KELLY, A & L GOODBODY

Introduction

Boardroom diversity, and more specifically, the representation of women on the boards of listed companies, is becoming an increasingly debated topic. The issue is complex, raising questions such as why, when women and men are equally successful as graduates and early in their careers, is there such a gender inequality on boards? Why is this of interest or importance to boards? Does it impact on the success or failure of businesses, and does the issue create a potential risk for listed companies?

This is a global issue, with some European countries such as Norway boasting 42 per cent of women on their boards, whilst the United States has considerably fewer at 16.1 per cent and China fewer again at 8 per cent.[1] In addition, legislative developments in the form of quotas from the European Commission are now in the pipeline.

Whether imposing mandatory quotas on listed companies is the most appropriate way to manage gender diversity is central to this discussion. Some argue that imposing a quota, with financial penalties for companies who fail to comply, is a necessary step to force companies to engage. The counter-argument from those who favour voluntary measures is that quotas may force a board to make a selection based on gender rather than merit. There is a need to align the quality of the candidate with the diversity agenda, and this is a real challenge facing boards.

This article examines the issue of gender diversity on boards and attempts to explore some of these questions, with reference to the UK Corporate Governance Code and the experience of boards in the UK and in Ireland.

Gender diversity: the barriers and obstacles explored

The most compelling and key study in this area in recent years was carried out in the UK by Lord Davies of Abersoch, who, in 2010, was commissioned by the UK government to identify the barriers preventing more women reaching the boardroom and to make recommendations about how to increase the proportion of women on corporate boards.

Davies reported his findings in 2011.[2] His report unearthed many of the complexities surrounding this issue and proved to be a catalyst for change, by recommending real and tangible measures to address the disparity that exists. Davies found that the low number of women on boards was, in part, 'a symptom of insufficient numbers emerging at the top of the management structure, and the under-representation of women in senior management generally'. He found that barriers to success included the informal networks which were influential on board appointments, the lack of transparency around selection criteria and the way in which executive search firms operated.

His report also highlighted that the drive to have an equal mix of male and female members on the boards of listed companies is moving away from the realms of political correctness based on gender equality, towards the increasingly-held view that gender diversity is an essential element of a successful corporation. He quoted evidence supporting the view that companies with a strong female representation at board and top management level perform better than those without,[3] and that gender-diverse boards have a positive impact on performance.

Davies also addressed the issues of why gender diversity should matter to the board and whether the issue impacts on a company's risk profile. He pointed to studies which demonstrate that a gender-balanced board is more likely to pay attention to managing and controlling risk,[4] and that having female directors on the board appears to lower a company's chances of bankruptcy.[5]

Some of the measures recommended by Davies included making changes to the Corporate Governance Code ('the Code'), which is issued by the Financial Reporting Council (FRC), and operates on a 'comply or explain' basis for listed companies in the UK. In Eire, the Code is followed by listed companies on the Main Securities Market of the Irish Stock Exchange.

The Code is comprised of a set of best practice principles for directors on the key components of effective board governance. The Code was published in 2010 and it replaced the Combined Code on Corporate Governance.

It should be said that in its original version in 2010, the Code was already leading the way on this issue as it recognized, for the first time, the value of diversity in the boardroom by stating that the search for board candidates should be conducted with 'due regard to the benefits of diversity'. However, of itself, this principle did not appear to be leading change at a sufficient pace.

The ante was therefore upped in 2012 when a revised version of the Code was published and one of Davies' recommendations was adopted among the changes. This required boards to become accountable by establishing a policy on boardroom diversity, including measurable objectives, and reporting annually on gender diversity within their corporation. Although Davies also called for a voluntary target of 25 per cent female representation on FTSE 100 boards by 2015, he declined to impose a quota on listed companies.

As a result of the changes introduced in the 2012 Code, gender diversity is now firmly on the agenda for listed companies, with prudent boards already taking or having taken the necessary steps to comply with both the spirit, as well as the letter, of these provisions of the Code.

The formal reporting requirement also raises the stakes for boards in terms of effective succession planning, and in ensuring that, from a risk perspective, the board is fit for purpose.

The UK Corporate Governance Code provisions on gender diversity: practical application by the board

There are three gender-diversity-specific provisions in the Code which boards should be aware of (emphasis added):

- *B2: Appointments to the Board.* There should be a formal, rigorous and transparent procedure for the appointment of new directors to the board (Main Principle). The search for board candidates should be conducted, and appointments made, on merit, against objective criteria and with due regard for the benefits of *diversity on the board including gender*. The board should satisfy itself that plans are in place for orderly succession for appointments to the board and to senior management, so as to maintain an appropriate balance of skills and experience within the company and on the board and to ensure progressive refreshing of the board.

- *B.2.4: Nomination committee.* A separate section of the annual report should describe the work of the nomination committee, including the process it has used in relation to board appointments. This section should include a description of the *board's policy on diversity, including gender*, any measurable objectives that it has set for implementing the policy and progress on achieving the objectives.

- *B6: Evaluation.* Evaluation of the board should consider the balance of skills, experience, independence and knowledge of the company on the board, *its diversity, including gender*, how the board works together as a unit, and other factors relevant to its effectiveness.

So how have listed companies in the UK responded to these requirements to date and has anything changed in practice?

In late 2013, the Cranfield International Centre for Women Leaders at Cranfield University (Cranfield) issued a report entitled *Women on Boards: Benchmarking adoption of the 2012 Corporate Governance Code in FTSE 350*, with the aim of monitoring progress on diversity reporting.[6] The Cranfield report indicated that, at the time of its publication, women accounted for 19 per cent of FTSE 100 and 15 per cent of FTSE 250 board positions – the highest level since Cranfield began monitoring the number of women in Britain's boardrooms in 1999. The report points out that this improvement is a result of what appears to be a cultural shift taking place within UK business.

Other findings of note were that 94 per cent of FTSE 100 companies now acknowledge the need for greater boardroom diversity and 65 per cent state that they have a clear policy to achieve this. The authors of the report state that whilst the majority of FTSE 100 companies indicated general support for the principle of diversity, this was not taken as evidence of a clear policy on boardroom diversity. Specific references to a stated or intended policy to increase boardroom diversity were required. Companies were required to demonstrate a proactive decision about, and commitment to, measurable objectives for gender diversity in the boardroom, rather than vague statements loosely agreeing in principle with Davies' aspirational target of 25 per cent women on boards. Overall, the Cranfield report found little change in diversity reporting by the FTSE 100 companies, compared to 2012.

However, in a sample of 50 FTSE 250 companies, the report indicated that while 82 per cent recognized the need for greater boardroom diversity, only 18 per cent stated a clear policy and just 14 per cent had set measurable objectives, although 24 per cent did address diversity in their board evaluation.

The report's authors conclude by urging companies to see compliance with the 2012 Code as an opportunity for improved corporate governance; to focus on outcomes rather than activities in monitoring their progress towards increased gender diversity in senior roles. Setting measurable objectives and sharing practices that appear to really work is crucial.

Succession planning for boards

One of the measures at the heart of this issue is succession planning and the ongoing need to appoint directors who fit the specific needs of the company and can make a positive contribution.

Succession planning is one of the key roles of the board and the FRC has issued *Guidance on Board Effectiveness*[7] ('the Guidance') which elaborates on this in detail. The Guidance states that the process of board recruitment should be continuous and proactive, and should take into account the company's agreed strategic priorities.

The Guidance outlines the personal attributes which should be considered when assessing diversity, including intellect, critical assessment and judgement, courage, openness, honesty and tact, the ability to listen, forge relationships and develop trust. Diversity of psychological type, background and gender are also important, to avoid establishing a board of like-minded individuals.

The challenge facing the board therefore is to balance the specific needs of the company with appointing the most appropriate directors, whilst considering the diversity objectives set out in the Guidance and the principles of the Code on board selection and gender diversity in particular. This balancing act creates the risk of a board making a gender-based appointment at the expense of selecting the best qualified and most suitable person for the role.

Baroness Hogg of the FRC recently commented that board succession was one of the issues most commonly identified by boards as in need of more attention when they assessed their own effectiveness.[8]

According to Baroness Hogg, succession planning needs to be broader than just developing a pipeline of female senior managers capable of serving on the board, but if companies can tackle this successfully it bodes well for the wider task.

Gender diversity and the Code: the Irish experience

Companies listed on the Main Securities Market of the Irish Stock Exchange also follow the UK Corporate Governance Code on a 'comply or explain' basis, along with an Irish Corporate Governance Annex to the Listing Rules. The Irish Corporate Governance Annex addresses the quality of disclosures in the areas of board composition, appointments, evaluation and re-election, and audit committees and remuneration.

Irish regulated credit institutions and insurance entities are required to follow the Central Bank of Ireland Corporate Governance Code (the CB Code) which exists on a statutory basis and, as a regulatory measure, its terms are mandatory rather than 'comply or explain' obligations. From January 2015, under the CB Code, boards or nomination committees will be required to establish a written policy on diversity, in line with the UK Corporate Governance Code.

The Institute of Directors in Ireland (the IOD) carried out a research project on women on boards in Ireland in 2013,[9] focusing in particular on the progress made and obstacles remaining. The report concluded, in line with Davies' experience in the UK, that a diverse board is more capable of understanding potential risks and identifying the impact of such risks to the business and its various stakeholders.

Respondents to the survey were asked why they believed the representation of women on boards of public listed companies was so low, at 9 per cent (compared to the EU average of 16 per cent). The survey showed that the three principle reasons for this were identified as:

- interlocking directorships in Ireland can mean that a small group of people populate boards and it can be difficult to break that chain;
- the lack of openness and transparency in board appointments; and
- women do not have access to predominantly male networks that bring them to the attention of chairpersons and nominations committees.

In terms of how to improve this, the majority of respondents said that a transparent, open and independent appointment process was crucial, along with rotation of long-serving directors. The key words emerging repeatedly from respondents on this topic were encouragement, support, mentoring, networks and education.

Interestingly, 81 per cent of respondents believed that women themselves should take some of the responsibility for the low level of women on boards in Ireland, with one respondent stating that women do not sufficiently support other women's advancement.

In terms of quotas, 29 per cent of respondents believed that gender quotas were the most effective means of increasing the number of women on boards, while 43 per cent believed that targets, rather than mandatory quotas, were preferable.

The reluctance to impose quotas was also a feature of a recent Central Bank of Ireland consultation on possible changes to the CB Code, with no support for a prescriptive approach such as quotas or targets to be applied or mandated.

Practical steps

In preparing for ongoing compliance with the UK Corporate Governance Code and Irish Annex principles, boards should be:

- preparing and regularly reviewing their written diversity policy, which should include gender;
- establishing a formal procedure for the appointment of new directors to the board, which should be transparent;
- ensuring that the search for new board candidates is conducted, and appointments made, on merit and using objective criteria and taking diversity, including gender, into account;
- ensuring that a separate section of the annual report describes the work of the nomination committee, including how board appointments are made and including details of the board's diversity policy and any measurable objectives used to implement the policy, along with details of progress made on achieving those objectives;
- focusing on planning future appointments to the board by linking succession planning with diversity so as to maintain an appropriate balance of skills, experience, independence and knowledge; and
- ensuring that board evaluation considers diversity, including gender, along with other factors relevant to the board's effectiveness.

Conclusion

Gender diversity is fast becoming a major board issue and the fact that gender quotas from the EU are in the pipeline only scores to underpin this.

Companies effectively have little choice now but to embrace the drive to have more women on their boards. Some commentators believe the drive is simply a logical one.[10]

Companies can ensure that their board continues to be fit for purpose by taking the required practical steps in the short term and above all, planning ahead in terms of future appointments. The nominee committee should drive this by refreshing their board search procedures and ensuring that any selection companies they use do the same. The committee should also ensure that the board consistently identifies senior talent within the organization with a view to filling future positions on the board.

Research has shown that a diverse board will readily and competently identify the potential risks to the company and the impact of those risks on the organization. It appears, therefore, that addressing this aspect of board composition is not merely a compliance issue but can offer real protection to the organization from a risk perspective.

Notes

1 Deloitte (March 2013) *Women in the Boardroom: a global perspective*, pp 4, 12

2 Lord Davies of Abersoch (February 2011) *Women on Boards*

3 McKinsey & Company (2007) *Women Matter*

4 *Diversity and Gender Balance in Britain plc*: a study by TCAM in conjunction with *The Observer* and as part of the Good Companies Guide, London, UK, TCAM 2009

5 Professor Nick Wilson, Leeds University Business School, 'Women in the boardroom help companies succeed', *The Times*, 19 March 2009

6 The Cranfield International Centre for Women Leaders at Cranfield University, *Women on Boards: Benchmarking adoption of the 2012 Corporate Governance Code in FTSE 350*

7 Financial Reporting Council (March 2011) *Guidance on Board Effectiveness*

8 The Cranfield International Centre for Women Leaders at Cranfield University, *Women on Boards: Benchmarking adoption of the 2012 Corporate Governance Code in FTSE 350*, p 5

9 Institute of Directors in Ireland (2013) *Women on boards in Ireland: Insights from women directors on the progress made and obstacles remaining*

10 Lucy Kellaway, *Financial Times* correspondent and FTSE 100 director, remarked in a recent article: 'You would have to be an idiot not to be in favour of this. For a company to limit itself to half the potential workforce makes no sense at all.' Citywire Money, March 2011

The future of UK pensions after the DWP's 'Defined Ambition' consultation

JAMES BORSHELL, DENTONS UKMEA LLP

Introduction

The Department for Work and Pensions (DWP) recently consulted[1] on a set of blue-sky proposals on the future shape of pensions in the United Kingdom.

In its consultation *Reshaping workplace pensions for future generations* the DWP accepts that traditional models of pension provision in the UK are no longer appropriate. It has asked the industry to consider three different pension structures that it has called 'Defined Ambition'. These new structures would represent a radical readjustment in the balance of risk between employers and workers in workplace pension provision.

So what is the UK traditional pensions model?

The UK private pension industry has two basic structures with clearly different risk profiles. The first structure is the *money purchase pension scheme*. This provides workers with an income in retirement based solely on what is in the worker's pension saving pot at retirement. The second structure is the *defined benefit pension* under which the scheme, and indirectly the worker's employer, promise to fund a guaranteed benefit for the worker at retirement.[2]

Money purchase pension schemes

Money purchase schemes are relatively simple to describe. They are sometimes referred to as 'defined contribution' schemes because the sole liability of the employer to provide to the worker's pension scheme is to pay in any agreed contributions.

Money purchase schemes can be provided via a trust, or via a contract with a personal pension provider. In either case the risk of a penurious retirement lies entirely with the worker. The size of the worker's 'pot' at retirement, which is used to buy the retirement pension, is determined by a number of elements, the most important being the amount paid in by the worker and their employer, the investment return on those contributions and the charges levied on the pot by the pensions provider.

No guarantees

Given the above it is easy to see there are no guarantees for workers with a money purchase pension.

It is possible to mitigate some of the investment risk using 'lifestyling'. Under this, the worker's pension pot is moved from riskier assets into government bonds and cash during the last few years before retirement. This removes the risk of falling foul of a short-term dip in the markets immediately before retirement but tends to reduce returns immediately before retirement.

The income the worker can buy using their pot usually depends on the annuity market.[3] Annuity rates are strongly linked to the assets that providers use to pay the worker's pension income. They have been in long-term decline due to market conditions in those assets. A glance at the financial pages will show that rates can vary wildly. Even workers with a relatively large pension pot could find themselves with a very limited income in retirement if they wish to protect themselves against inflation, provide spouse benefits etc.

Because of this, money purchase schemes tend to be viewed negatively by workers, but positively by employers. They are also currently the preferred solution for most employers to meet the DWP's 'auto-enrolment' requirements. Under these, workers will be automatically enrolled into a pension scheme to start them off on pensions saving, which makes their flaws all the more serious.

Defined benefit pension schemes

The standard form of defined benefit pension scheme in the UK is a final salary scheme, although recently it has been increasingly replaced with 'career average' or 'CARE' schemes.

Final salary schemes provide an income at retirement for the employee based on a proportion of their final salary multiplied by years of service under the scheme.

Other variants of the defined benefit model include:

- The CARE model provides a pension based on a proportion of each year's actual salary, rather than on the final salary.

- Cash balance schemes promise a fixed 'pot' and/or fixed annuity rates to provide certainty in either the amount of the pension pot or the annuity that can be provided at retirement.

In each case any shortfall in the assets to be used to meet this liability falls on the employer. Many employers have been increasing employee contributions, or introducing cost-sharing mechanisms to keep costs down.

Breaking the camel's back

The high point of defined benefit pension schemes in the UK was at the end of the 1970s, followed by a slow decline as costs mounted. The reasons for this are relatively clear. An employer in the 1970s would have been faced with the following risks:

- *Salary increases*: workers' salaries tend to be higher at the end of their careers than at the start; therefore the rate of salary increase over workers' careers is an important consideration.
- *Investment returns*: in much the same situation as a worker with a money purchase scheme, employers have to hope the returns on their investments will meet their liabilities to the scheme.
- *Longevity*: the longer the worker lives in retirement, the longer the scheme will need to pay a pension. Longevity assumptions could be worked into the funding of the scheme and were partially supported by new workers coming into schemes to fund them during their working lives.

Since the 1970s, tax changes have reduced the assets available to meet the scheme liabilities,[4] whilst liabilities have been increased[5] through a variety of legislative changes imposed on pension schemes to meet social concerns:

- *Preservation*. Any worker who is a member of a defined benefit scheme and who leaves service with at least two years of pensionable service needs to have their pension benefits preserved in the scheme. This means that they must be given a pension at retirement based on their salary at departure.
- *Revaluation in deferment*. With effect from 1 January 1986, the worker's preserved benefits need to be revalued by the inflation rate with an initial cap of 5 per cent, although this has since been reduced as the associated costs in a low-inflation, low-returns environment became apparent in the mid-2000s.
- *Indexation in payment*. In 1997 the government introduced inflation protection for pensions in payment in respect of benefits accrued on and after 6 April 1997. Similar provisions already applied to guaranteed minimum pensions – a way that employers could save on their national insurance by providing a part of the state pension in an occupational scheme.
- *Barber*. Under the Barber judgment, schemes need to provide equalized normal pension ages for men and women. In practice this means that schemes

with a 60/65 pension age split, mirroring the former state pension ages, have to lower their normal pension age for men to 60 until they can amend their scheme to provide for a higher one.

- *Scheme funding*. From 6 April 1997 the government introduced a requirement for employers to fund their pension schemes at the 'minimum funding requirement'. This was increased in 2006 to funding at the 'scheme specific funding' level. The 2006 legislation provided that any shortfalls in funding had to be made up via recovery plans enforced by the Pensions Regulator over a 'reasonable period' of time.

- *Pension Protection Fund levies*. The Pension Protection Fund (PPF) was introduced to protect members whose schemes wound up with a deficit and no employer able to meet that deficit. In order to meet this admirable aim the PPF takes in the assets of schemes in this situation and also charges a levy on all other defined benefit schemes to meet its liabilities.

Coupled with pension enhancements agreed to meet the government's rules on surpluses, designed to avoid having productive capital locked up in pension schemes, it is easy to see why today's defined benefit schemes are underfunded.

The DWP's proposals

The risk allocation under the current system is clearly weighted at two extremes: either the worker faces all the risks, or the employer faces all the risks. The DWP's proposals seek to strike a balance between these two extremes and thereby reinvigorate UK pensions: the first proposal by lifting some of the weight from an employer with a defined benefit scheme; the second and third by removing the risk associated with money purchase schemes from the worker.

The wider context for the proposals is auto-enrolment. The DWP is likely to be worried that it could face challenges similar to those it faced in respect of the failure of the minimum funding requirement, and pensions mis-selling scandals, where workers are put into a poor value pension scheme under legislative mandate.

Flexible defined benefit

Flexible defined benefit is proposed as the 'defined benefit light' option. Defined benefit pensions would be paid and much of the existing legal framework would be retained. However, pensions in payment would no longer need to be indexed for inflation. Instead inflation increases or lump sum increases would be discretionary and paid only where the funding of the scheme permitted. This would mirror the situation under many older pension schemes.

Other proposals include:

- Removing the requirement to retain preserved benefits in the scheme, instead of which an early leaver would receive a transfer value that they could take to their new employer.

- Allowing employers to change a scheme's normal pension age to reflect changes in longevity assumptions. This would mean that employers would not face a sudden increase in their funding due to changes in assumptions about how long their workforce might live.

Taken together these changes would reduce the level of risk assumed by an employer for new schemes. The DWP has also suggested that employers with existing defined benefit schemes could switch to 'DB light' for future accrual to save costs.

These suggestions represent an acknowledgement that employers who are willing to provide a guarantee of a good income for their workers in retirement should not be required to run their business into the ground in order to do so due to circumstances beyond their control.

Adding certainty to defined contribution: defined contribution with guarantees

The second option is a variant of the money purchase scheme, where a third party provides a guarantee for the workers that their pension pot will not be wiped out immediately before retirement. The DWP's proposals for this have four basic 'flavours':

- A defined contribution scheme in which the worker's pension savings pot at retirement would never fall below the amount paid into it by the member, plus any employer contributions.

- An industry-standardized capital and investment return guarantee, to be purchased by a fiduciary on behalf of multiple scheme members from insurers or similar providers.

- Retirement income insurance bought by a fiduciary on the worker's behalf each year from the age of 50 using the member's pension savings fund. At retirement, the worker would take a pension directly from their pension savings. Where the savings run out, the insurance would kick in and start paying a retirement income, thereby avoiding the risk of a worker running out of money in retirement.

- A split pension savings pot, with a proportion used to buy a deferred nominal annuity and payable from the member's pension age. This would give the worker a clear and identifiable pension income, which would run in parallel with the remainder of their pot. This remainder could go into a collective higher-risk set of investments to provide future indexation.

The main issue with these proposals is where these guarantees would come from, and how much they would cost. A basic contributions guarantee would be unlikely to be too expensive, but the value of it would be very limited. The capital and investment guarantee could well end up being as expensive as a formal defined benefit scheme. It also looks surprisingly like the existing cash balance schemes mentioned above, which already exist, but which have so far proven relatively unpopular.

Retirement insurance appears to be an interesting idea but would require an industry adjustment to provide these new products. Again, the question of pricing looms. If the cost of this insurance ate appreciably into the worker's pension pot, then the net effect might be negative overall. In the current market, the last idea, split pension annuity purchases, could fall foul of the fact that small pots of money buy very bad annuity rates. Splitting an annuity purchase into tranches may again have a detrimental effect on pensions incomes.

Going Dutch: collective defined contribution

The final proposal is a variant of the Dutch collective defined contribution scheme structure.

This involves large pooled funds that benefit from the lower costs associated with scale. They also allow members to reduce the risk that when they come to retirement there will be a dip in the investments they hold. This structure also allows for clear targeted pensions incomes given that the worker's pension is partially funded by ongoing contributions from other workers in the scheme.

This is obviously attractive and the Dutch system is well regarded. Even though it has recently been having some funding issues, the structure allows retirement incomes to be adjusted to reflect this as target incomes are not guaranteed.

Given that there is a working version of this system already in place, and the general push from the Pensions Regulator towards larger, more efficient schemes, this seems the most likely of the money purchase options to receive follow-up. It is also likely to be easier to sell to workers. One of the main problems that auto-enrolment was intended to address was the drop in the number of workers saving for their retirements since the slow demise of the defined benefit system began.[6]

Summing up

Given the current 'all or nothing' approach to risk represented by the money purchase/ defined benefit pensions dichotomy in the UK, it is clear that some alternatives need to be provided. The general approach in the consultation is that the regulatory framework for the new pensions would be less prescriptive and legislation driven, and more concerned with what actually works in practice.

Looking at the specific proposals, it is unlikely that the defined benefit light option will reinvigorate the defined benefit market. Arguably, it is simply too little too late. The option to convert existing schemes to defined benefit light may be popular with the few employers still offering this type of provision, whether from paternalistic or practical competitive reasons.

On the other hand, the money purchase options could represent a new dawn for UK private pensions. They appear to be based on the premise that if you open the market up to competition then innovative products tend to appear. Given an effective regulatory environment, workers' income put into a money purchase scheme would no longer be faced with the risk of a penniless retirement. As noted, the Dutch system is already operating and is the subject of quite a lot of admiring comment from other national systems.

Given the positive elements of the proposal the main question is whether the DWP can get its legislative proposals in place before the next election.[7] However, it is to be hoped that in this one area there may be a general recognition across the political spectrum that the status quo simply is not working.

Notes

1 https://www.gov.uk/government/uploads/system/uploads/attachment_data/file/255541/reshaping-workplace-pensions-for-future-generations.pdf

2 See section 181 of the Pension Schemes Act 1993 for the definition of 'money purchase benefits'.

3 Although income drawdown has been a long-term option since 2011, the number of workers able to access it is relatively limited due to the pension savings limits applicable.

4 See as an example http://www.ft.com/cms/s/0/e6ae9368-eee1-11e2-b8ec-00144feabdc0.html#axzz2sGidLTLO

5 For a more detailed list of the pensions changes in the modern pensions system I would suggest http://www.pensionsadvisoryservice.org.uk/pensions-timeline

6 http://www.ons.gov.uk/ons/rel/pensions/pension-trends/chapter-6–private-pensions–2013-edition/art-chp6-2013.html#tab-The-changing-landscape

7 http://www.parliament.uk/about/how/elections-and-voting/general/general-election-timetable-2015

Making yourself heard in redundancy consultation and termination meetings

**HENRIETTA WATCHORN AND DAVID WHINCUP,
SQUIRE SANDERS (UK) LLP**

It will come as no great surprise that the majority of managers would rather do almost anything other than deliver a difficult message to someone in their team. According to research carried out by the Centre for Effective Dispute Resolution, over a third of managers would rather parachute jump for the first time, whilst some 27 per cent would prefer to shave their head for charity.

In the challenging economic climate of recent years, an increasing number of managers have been faced with telling one or more of their team that they are 'at risk' of redundancy or that they are indeed redundant. These meetings are not easy for anyone. Delivering these messages is hard, and delivering it to someone who is tearful and emotional, unresponsive or puce with rage is harder still. Needless to say, the impact upon the individual receiving that message can be catastrophic. This chapter focuses on preparing for such meetings, delivering that difficult message and ensuring, as best you can, that you are heard.

The legal bit

In the UK, redundancy is one of the five potentially fair reasons for dismissal and section 139 of the Employment Rights Act 1996 sets out the statutory definition.

In essence, an employee is redundant if his dismissal is wholly or mainly attributable to the fact that there has been:

1 a closure of a business for the purposes of which the employee was employed; or

2 a closure of a workplace where the employee was employed; or

3 a reduced requirement for employees to carry out work of a particular kind or to do so at the place where he was employed to work.

In order for a dismissal to be fair it must fall within the statutory definition and a fair process must also be followed. Consultation with the employee about the proposed redundancy is fundamental to the fairness of any dismissal, and although the legislation does not set out prescribed timescales within which consultation with individuals should take place, the shorter the consultation period, the more likely that it will be called into question. Only once the consultation process is complete, including any search for suitable alternative employment, should an employee's employment be terminated.

Preparation is key

A report published in 2012 by Dr Ian Ashman, Institute for Research into Organisations, Work and Employment, University of Central Lancashire, suggests that the vast majority of those tasked with delivering the redundancy message considered it to be the most emotionally demanding thing they had undertaken in their working lives. There is absolutely nothing wrong with being nervous or apprehensive (indeed if you feel nothing at all, you are probably not really suited to handling these things) but going into such a meeting underprepared is a sure-fire way to get off to a bad start. The Advisory Conciliation and Arbitration Service (ACAS) has produced guidance entitled *Challenging conversations and how to manage them*, available via its website, which provides some helpful advice on how to deal with difficult conversations.

What am I doing here?

At the outset, you need to know whether you are informing or consulting, as these are very different things at law and occur at different stages of the process. Essentially you will be either:

1 telling the employee that he is at risk and then adjourning quickly so he can make representations at a later consultation meeting; or

2 hearing those representations and any questions he may have; or

3 delivering the news that he is being dismissed for redundancy.

Make sure you know which it is!

In the initial 'at risk' meeting (where the employee is notified that his role is being placed at risk of redundancy) and at any further consultation meeting, the redundancy is merely a proposal and you should invite the employee's views and representations on ways in which the redundancy might be avoided and so forth. To avoid confusing the message, be careful with your language: use 'would' rather than 'will', and ensure that repeated references are made to 'proposed, intended, possible, provisional, current thinking' etc. This will be harder if you know the redundancy to be actually or all but decided upon already, but in such cases it is doubly important to pick your terminology carefully so that the subconscious mind does not let this slip out.

The 'informing' part (the redundancy termination meeting) should take place only once the consultation process is complete and any search for suitable alternative roles has failed. At this stage of the process, it is not necessary to invite the employee's views but the redundancy decision should be confirmed in writing and the employee notified of his right to appeal the decision in line with the ACAS Code of Practice and any internal policy.

Before any such meeting, it is essential that you clearly plan what you are going to say. You should not be afraid of referring to a pre-prepared script, as it will not only help you to remain in control, but also ensure that all of the key points are covered. You cannot predict how an employee will react and having a script in front of you will help you bring the meeting back to the key points if it goes off on a tangent. You should ensure that you are aware of, and adhere to, any internal company policy that governs the redundancy process in order to ensure that a fair process is followed.

It is also essential that you are able to clearly explain the business rationale for the proposed redundancy. The employee may have questions about the selection criteria, who made the decision, and so forth, and it will be a far easier meeting if you have this information at your fingertips. But three tips here: first, the script should ideally be bullet-pointed only, and not text. If you simply read something out loud it will sound mechanical and careless of the individual's own position. Second, the script will be a disclosable document, so write nothing on it before or during the meeting which would be awkward if seen by the employee. Last, if you get questions which you cannot answer, don't guess – note them down and promise to revert later.

If you are in the difficult position of having to place a number of individuals at risk of redundancy at the same time, it is important to ensure that you schedule time for a break between each of the meetings. Not only is there the risk that the meetings will overrun (cutting a consultation meeting short for 'the next one' just looks dreadful, even if objectively everything useful has already been said), but you should not underestimate how emotionally draining such meetings can be. If you feel that you require additional support or training then you should ask your employer to provide this. ACAS recommends that it should be made available to you.

The meeting

How should I start the meeting?

It may sound obvious, but the first few minutes of such a meeting are likely to set the tone for the rest. Something as simple as asking the individual if they would like some water is likely to get you off to a better start than a potentially loaded question such as 'How are you?' It goes without saying that the meeting should take place somewhere you will not be disturbed. You should have a note-taker present to make sure that everything discussed is recorded. The notes need not be verbatim, but you should try to ensure that an accurate note is taken of all the main points raised at the meeting so as to lessen the risk of later argument about what was or was not said.

Who can accompany the employee at the meeting?

Under section 10 of the Employment Relations Act 1999, workers have a statutory right to be accompanied at a consultation meeting by a colleague or a recognized trade union official. This excludes the initial meeting where the employee is told he is at risk, and the final one where he is given notice; so it applies principally to the actual consultation meeting in the middle, where he gets to make his arguments in response to the proposal. In order to trigger this right, a worker must 'reasonably request' to be accompanied at the meeting. The recent Employment Appeal Tribunal (EAT) case of *Toal & Anor v GB Oils Ltd* (2013) considered whether the word 'reasonably' applies to the choice of representative as well as the request itself? No, according to the EAT in *Toal*. In its view, provided that a worker has asked to be accompanied by a colleague or trade union representative, an employer cannot reject the employee's request to be accompanied, even if it has concerns about the chosen representative. In other words, workers have an absolute right to choose their companion, subject to the safeguard set out in the legislation that the companion is a colleague or trade union official.

It is best practice to ask an employee for the name of his representative. That said, not all employees will comply with such a request. Sometimes the identity of the representative will be obvious (for example, when it is another employee) but in other cases it may be far from clear. In these circumstances you would be within your right to suspend the meeting pending confirmation of the identity of the individual. However, there may be some occasions where although it is technically outside the scope of the statutory requirements (for example, the individual has brought along a lawyer or family member) the meeting may in fact be more productive (and your message more effectively delivered) by allowing that person to attend.

What should I do if an employee asks to record the meeting?

Very few people like the sound of their own voice (there are exceptions, of course) and the thought of being recorded often unnerves even the most seasoned public speakers. However, as a general rule, it is always best to imagine that all such meetings are being recorded. (After all, we are all more likely to behave in our most professional manner if there is a chance that our boss or the tribunal might listen to said tape!)

You would be within your rights to object to the meeting being recorded (offer a pad and a pen instead), but there is always the risk that the employee covertly records the meeting anyway. In *Vaughan v London Borough of Lewisham* (2013) the EAT refused permission for Mrs Vaughan to use 39 hours of covert recordings in evidence, but noted that just because a recording had been made covertly (and indeed dishonestly

– she had expressly assured her employer that she was not taping the meeting), this did not by itself make it inadmissible. If at a later date you discover that a meeting has been recorded, you should request a copy of the recording and any transcript as soon as possible, and not assume that because it was recorded without your knowledge it will be inadmissible as evidence.

What if the employee becomes antagonistic or accusatory?

It is impossible to forecast how any given employee might react to the news of potential or actual redundancy but if he or she becomes irate or antagonistic you should avoid the temptation to argue points there and then. A useful tactic is imagining that you are in a tank (armoured, not fish); if you remain inside the tank, then whatever the employee fires at you will bounce off the shell, whereas if you get out of the tank and enter into hand-to-hand combat, it is far more likely that you will get hurt. In a redundancy context, you are far better listening to what the employee is saying rather than instantly reacting to or arguing with the points that are being made. You are then less likely to make a response in the heat of the moment, and can instead reflect on the meeting notes and what has been said, thereby delivering a more reasoned response later. That said, if the employee becomes overly aggressive, you should adjourn the meeting for a brief period so that you can both settle down, and you should record your reasons for doing so in the meeting notes.

How do I end the meeting?

This will depend on whether it is a consultation meeting or the meeting in which you inform the individual that their role is redundant. At the end of a consultation meeting, you should ask the employee if they have anything at all further to add. At the redundancy termination meeting this is not necessary (though they may have questions) but instead you will need to inform the employee that the decision will be confirmed in writing.

On a practical note, after the meeting has concluded you might consider arranging transport home for the affected employee, or perhaps ensuring that there is a place for them to sit privately and collect themselves before getting behind the wheel. If you are sending the employee home on pay pending the next meeting, make sure he or she understands that this is a suspension only (NB **not** 'garden leave', which technically applies post-notice only), and not a dismissal.

Making yourself heard in consultation meetings

People react very differently to the R-word. There are some who greet the news with anger or distress, others who come armed with a list of questions and half-comprehended snippets of legal advice clearly gleaned from Google, those who do not speak at all, and the rare few who may in fact be genuinely pleased about the news. Undeniably, however, the individual on the receiving end of that message is liable to be het up (in one way or another) about the news. (I took part in a redundancy training session role-play for a client some months ago, tearfully announcing at the start of the 'at risk' meeting that I was pregnant. Even though the client's manager dealt admirably with this particular curve-ball, and even though I was not genuinely at risk, tearful **or** pregnant, I **still** had difficulties hearing past 'redundancy'.)

Where employees do become stressed or distressed or silent in such a meeting, great care needs to be taken to ensure that they understand what has (and often as importantly, has not) just happened. It is too easy for them to hear the R-word and then mentally shut down, extrapolating forward in an instant to their mortgage, the school fees, credit card repayments, unemployment, divorce and homelessness, while whatever you are saying becomes just background noise. So take it gently. Repeat the key points as often as you need – that no final decision has been made, that scope for redeployment may exist or (at a pinch) that there will be a financial cushion available. Remember that you are in control of the meeting and there is nothing wrong with adjourning the meeting for a short break. It is a brutal business which nothing can make painless, but do try not to let your own anxieties lead you to lose focus on what is being heard or digested by the employee. This may be either very much less or very much more than the words you actually use and it will often pay just to check his or her understanding before the meeting wraps up.

Conveying the right message to the rest of your workforce

The employees left behind after redundancy rounds are very often forgotten about. Frog-marching the redundant staff out of the building is unlikely to garner support or instil a sense of loyalty in the survivors. You may not be able to give the rest of the team a cast-iron guarantee that there will be no more redundancies in the coming months, or any kind of financial incentive, but ensuring that the individual who is being made redundant is seen to be treated with respect (as opposed to being asked to clear their desk in five minutes) will convey a far better message to the remaining employees.

Redundancy decisions are unfortunately a way of life, but this does not negate the need for such messages to be delivered in as clear and sensitive a manner as possible, whilst ensuring that it is not so sugar-coated that the employee walks away with the wrong message entirely. There is no necessary inconsistency between clarity on the one hand and sensitivity or empathy on the other. For your own sake, let alone that of the employee, ensure that you know in advance what you are doing, why and what happens next. If you are unclear in your own mind on these things, it will be little surprise if your message in the redundancy meeting is not properly heard.

PART FOUR
Managing risk in emerging markets

Environmental risk in emerging markets

GAVIN O'TOOLE

Introduction

In 2011, a court in Ecuador fined the US oil major Chevron a breathtaking $19 billion for environmental damage caused in the country's Amazon region since the 1960s by Texaco, which merged with Chevron in 2001. Environmental and indigenous organizations that had been campaigning against the corporation for 17 years applauded the decision – later reduced to $9 billion – in a case that indicated how assertive countries and political groups in Latin America and the Caribbean are becoming in pressing environmental claims against large companies.

The decision was the latest twist in a tortuous legal saga between Chevron and 30,000 Ecuadoreans that had its origins way back in 1967 when Texaco first struck oil in the country. Chevron fought the claim vigorously, for 10 years bogging it down in lawsuits in the United States itself, but by 2011 had exhausted the patience of the US court system. The corporation duly denounced the Ecuadorean rulings as illegitimate and politicized, fanning the flames of Latin American hostility towards it. And the most important environmental case of the 21st century continued, with Chevron returning to the US courts after turning on the lawyers that have fought Ecuador's corner.

The case is a stark example of the potential risks posed by environmental disputes to companies that operate in developing regions such as Latin America, and how political institutions once routinely dismissed as ineffective are now more willing, under public pressure, to take on the corporate giants they once courted uncritically.

It also reveals key characteristics of environmental risk which the Institute of Risk Management (IRM), among others, classifies as a miscellaneous 'emergent' risk characterized by fluidity and uncertainty. Chevron's struggle was as political as it was legalistic; it proved to be a poor communicator; it misunderstood how the public interpret liability; and it has seemed oblivious to the reputational damage such disputes can cause in the emerging markets that are so important for it.

Environmental risks faced by foreign investors in the developing world continue to be understood largely as emergent within a framework of analysis stunted by the difficulties risk managers face in anticipating environmental problems. Perhaps the most obvious example of an emergent risk is climate change, a theme that has risen up the agenda of business relentlessly. In July 2013, for example, the Center for Climate and Energy Solutions in Washington reported that most global S&P100 companies see extreme weather and other climate change impacts as current or near-term business risks, and that more than one-third had already experienced the adverse effects of these.[1] The Multilateral Investment Guarantee Agency, the World Bank Group's risk insurance arm, has applied comprehensive social and environmental performance standards to its projects for many years; yet its own research indicates that among the dimensions of political risk of most concern to investors, the environment does not figure.[2] Moreover, there are few systematic scholarly analyses of the political risks generated by environmental issues.

This is doubly surprising: the Chevron case and many like it demonstrate that environmental disputes are a growing source of political conflict in the developing world; and the importance attributed by economists to foreign direct investment in emerging economies and to the role played by private finance in development has grown dramatically.

All companies are subject to the costs and liabilities of environmental exposures, but a distinction can be made between ecosystem and organizational risk: the former encapsulates issues of environmental hazard and questions of liability that can be assigned a monetary value and dealt with through insurance; the latter has a bearing on the public image or reputation of an organization and – notwithstanding political risk insurance – can only be dealt with as a strategic issue that places an emphasis on review and communication. In emerging economies, a cohort of factors pushing environmental issues up the political agenda should make these a priority consideration for risk managers and suggest that it is more important than ever to understand the underlying political context and tensions within emerging markets surrounding issues such as land use and resource control. The site dependency of environmental risks in the developing world will not just be exacerbated by variation in legal controls in different states, but by socio-political dynamics that are rapidly transforming attitudes and perceptions of the environment itself. Democratization, institutional reform, changing modes of representation, multilateral influences on policymaking and new ideas are all interacting to complicate analysis.

Latin America provides a regional focus that offers ways of understanding how green issues interact with traditional political risk factors in the developing world. A snapshot of popular mobilization against large development projects in the region reveals extensive social movement activism in support of environmental causes – opposition to the construction of roads and hydroelectric dams, action against deforestation, and mobilization against large-scale mining. Often, the corporations at the heart of these disputes suffer both reputational damage and financial loss for failing to foresee issues that subsequently generate green heat. Such is the prominence that environmental disputes are gaining in Latin America, that they are transforming it into a laboratory of green politics. This chapter identifies and explores these with the aim of offering some broad contextual insights for risk managers.

Environmental risk in developing regions: Latin America

The management of environmental issues is a key concern for most companies and can make or break a brand's reputation. Many methodologies exist for managing environmental risk, yet many companies still fail to see green issues coming, and scepticism persists among some sectors of the corporate world and political circles about the environmental implications of development and about climate change. This reflects the politicized nature of green issues today as well as what environmental thinkers call the 'traditional paradigm' in policy making that advocates perpetual growth. It may also reflect organizational factors such as poor cooperation between environmental and other corporate functions; inadequate systems for identifying environmental issues; and an emphasis on compliance rather than planning.

Environmental risk analysis has traditionally sought to estimate the probability of an adverse impact on the environment resulting from human activity, and a science of empirically quantifying risk has developed to set the scene for risk management policies. Nonetheless, the characteristics of environmental goods – often seen as 'public goods' that we all have a stake in protecting but are nonetheless rarely costed – can set such risks apart by making the cost/benefit analysis of risk problematic. This helps to explain why environmental risks are intrinsically reputational, because they generate public concern related to issues of health and livelihoods. Given this, perhaps more than any other category of risk, environmental risk needs to be considered by managers in ways that address its political, social and economic implications.

This injunction is magnified in the developing world, where communities facing man-made hazards tend to be marginalized, meaning the balance of power is rarely in their favour. They are unable to speak in scientific language and have little or no representation or access to mass communication – and so invariably devolve a key role to more politicized actors. Factors such as these help to explain why two key principles are prominent in the approach taken by public authorities in the developing world to assessing and governing environmental risk: the precautionary principle, whereby a lack of scientific certainty should not be used as a reason for postponing preventative measures; and the associated notion that the polluter pays, that is, users of environmental resources must prevent and mitigate damage they may cause through various strategies of remediation.

A large body of prescriptive material has evolved in the field of environmental risk assessment and management which, generally, aims to minimize liability in order to protect a company's assets, financial health, property and reputation. Tools that can help companies identify and avoid environmental liabilities include environmental audits; understanding of laws and regulations; and savvy communication, an issue complicated by the fact that risk perceptions vary. In making decisions, risk managers are often advised by government agencies to consider social, economic, political or legal issues alongside risk assessment results, and to incorporate public opinion and political demands into decision making. There has duly been a much greater effort to combine qualitative with quantitative forms of risk analysis and adopt more inclusive processes. Research by the ClimateWise initiative at the University of

Cambridge Programme for Sustainability Leadership – the global insurance industry's leadership group to drive action on climate change risk – argues that over the last few years there has been an increase in coordinated efforts to encourage the integration of environmental, social and governance factors into valuation and investment decisions.

Latin America and the Caribbean offer many examples that attest to the importance of such themes in managing environmental risk, and hence the pressing need to consider social and political contexts. A key characteristic of this part of the world is socio-economic and ethnic diversity, which greatly complicate the challenges of applying a one-size-fits all commercial strategy, and diversity also characterizes its physical and natural environment. Foreign corporations invariably access this region through interlocutors in the urban 'modern' sector, usually in capital cities, yet many of the environmental disputes there are confined to remote areas, where abundant natural resources are ripe for exploitation, inhabited by ethnically distinct groups who may not even speak Spanish or Portuguese.

The environmental issues discussed below have risen rapidly up agendas across Latin America as a result of a complex interaction of political developments following democratization in the 1980s.

Institutions and policies in flux

Environmental governance in Latin America has developed rapidly over the last 20 years as governments incorporate green concerns into public administration through a dynamic process of institution building. Some elements of this new institutional landscape have, in turn, enhanced the growth of environmentalism as a theme in politics, such as 'judicialization', whereby growing judicial independence has meant that courts are now assertively determining the outcomes of environmental disputes; and decentralization, which is increasingly vesting environmental responsibilities in semi-autonomous agencies or state, departmental or municipal councils. A strong traditional emphasis on constitutionalism has meant the environment is becoming a major theme of ongoing constitutional reform in the region. At the same time, environmental institutions in Latin America face specific problems deriving from the region's political history, not least rapid and poorly planned institutional change, unevenness in how environmental law is applied within a country, a lack of authority and legal clarity, and 'regulatory capture' whereby an agency responsible for regulations is dominated by commercial interests that can conflict with the public interest. Behind these institutions, policy makers in Latin America have approached environmental issues according to the traditional policy paradigm, giving priority to economic growth over environmental protection, resulting in the creation of environment ministries weak in comparison with economic ministries. This has meant that political as opposed to technical criteria often determine how environmental policy tools are used. International trends also play a disproportionately important role in Latin American regulation.

Economic policy instruments are often seen as a more efficient alternative to regulation in environmental policy making, from traditional government spending to instruments that aim to harness market forces (market-based instruments or

'MBIs') that include eco-taxes, effluent charges, cap-and-trade systems, liability rules and tradable permits. But MBIs face considerable challenges and can sometimes be difficult to implement: in Latin America, for example, tax enforcement historically has been lax and large sections of the population survive outside the formal economy. Corruption also complicates enforcement, and government initiatives can be poorly targeted and badly monitored, and can be hijacked by political interests. Other constraints on the implementation of policies include legal formalism, administrative backwardness, and limited access to reliable information about the environment.

A growing green political lobby

One of the most important developments in the politics of Latin America and the Caribbean has been growing political mobilization around environmental issues. The region is mostly still consolidating democracy after decades of authoritarian rule, and democratization has placed parties at the heart of politics and provided new spaces for green activism. New green parties and indigenous movements are finding it easier than ever before to spearhead an environmental agenda, which has also been embraced by existing parties. The rise of centrist politics in fast-growing consumer societies is challenging the traditional left and right, forcing them to embrace a post-modern agenda that includes environmentalism. A good example of this development came in October 2010 in Brazil when Marina Silva, a former environment minister running as the Partido Verde (PV, Green Party) candidate, unexpectedly polled almost 20 per cent of the vote in the first round of the country's presidential elections. An equally important development has been the rise of indigenous parties in Ecuador, Bolivia, Colombia, Venezuela and Peru, for whom the environment offers a potent focus for other claims.

Beyond their ecological commitments and criticisms of development models, several features recur in the platforms of these new parties, but a key emphasis is often on the economic equality and sustainable development more traditionally associated with the old left, largely because of persistently high levels of poverty and inequality. Alongside parties, much environmental activism in Latin America has taken place outside the formal realms of politics among social groups, some of which have professionalized rapidly and lobby policymakers and corporations. These often gain the support of well-funded domestic and international NGOs, which give them technical and practical support. Social movements in Latin America employ a diverse range of tactics, from direct action and mass protest to conventional lobbying. Brand image and company social responsibility policies offer activists new opportunities to place corporations under pressure. In 2004, for example, indigenous Ecuadoreans addressed the annual shareholder meeting of the oil company Burlington Resources in Texas to demand that it halt exploration in the rainforest. This example also illustrates how environmental campaigns in Latin America are increasingly transnational, reflecting alliances between organizations across frontiers and the cross-border nature of many environmental disputes. Brazil has been a high priority of international NGOs because of the perceived link between deforestation and climate change.

The rising prominence of the environment in international relations

The global profile assumed by the Amazon rainforest in debates about climate change is evidence of how some of our most pressing environmental challenges transcend traditional approaches to international relations. The environment as an issue has been giving Latin America and the Caribbean a global profile since the 1992 Earth Summit in Rio de Janeiro. The region is also undergoing rapid globalization, which is testing traditional understandings of sovereignty hostile to external interference in the domestic affairs of a nation state, a view that has long been a defining characteristic of Latin American foreign relations. The determination of governments to defend sovereignty remains a bone of contention in environmental diplomacy: Latin American countries often bridle at suggestions about how they exploit their resources. Environmental problems do not respect national frontiers, meaning conservation strategies today emphasize cooperation, and problems once considered sub-regional – such as deforestation and water shortages – are now seen as international. Globalization has also removed barriers to trade and investment, with huge implications for the environment, and a key feature of trade opening in Latin America has been the proliferation of regional integration initiatives such as NAFTA, which inaugurated the trend for incorporating environmental 'side-agreements' in bilateral trade deals. In response to this, fears about competitiveness are behind clauses written into a number of free trade agreements in the region that strengthen the ability of a corporation to sue a government for damages caused by environmental regulations. Globalization is also fostering multilateralism, and Latin American states increasingly pursue common positions towards international environmental agreement, and a large number of international rules comprising what is broadly referred to as international environmental law have been accepted throughout the region.

Impact of climate change

Upon these recent political developments in Latin America can be superimposed the dramatic potential implications of climate change. The region is not considered to be a main contributor of greenhouse gases, yet will be disproportionately affected by them. Climate change threatens to exacerbate extreme weather events, land-use issues, deforestation, ecosystem change and biodiversity loss, stress to marine and freshwater resources and the many problems already faced by growing 'megacities'. It is also likely to have broader political and economic consequences, affecting primary production such as agriculture, livestock raising and fisheries. A study compiled for the Rio+20 summit in 2012 warned that the region faces annual damages of $100 billion by 2050.[3] Losses caused by disasters and more frequent extreme weather could undermine growth and frustrate poverty reduction, threatening economic assets and pushing up the cost of doing business. Climate change will affect trade, manufacturing, tourism and the insurance industry as well as energy generation and distribution. It is also likely to affect political systems by exacerbating poverty and inequality, thereby intensifying pressure on natural resources and deepening gender and ethnic inequalities. Urban policy makers will have to confront growing challenges to ensure the continuity of basic services, and the problems faced by cities in particular may deepen an existing urban bias in politics.

Given this, Latin American and Caribbean governments have begun to develop their own distinctive analysis of climate change and how to respond to international initiatives seeking low-carbon development. The growing prominence of this issue has also fostered widespread official support for the notion of sustainable development, and the UN conference to mark the 20th anniversary of the Rio Earth summit held in Brazil in 2012 aimed to renew political commitment to this theme. The pursuit of sustainable development has political implications for developing regions such as Latin America because the notion of the 'green economy' implies the need to maintain a balance between all the stakeholders in it: governments, civil society and the private sector. This means more effort may be required to reduce poverty and inequality by distributing more equally the income gained from exploiting the natural resources on which growth is currently based. Sustainable development initiatives and clean tech offer scope for job creation, which could encourage greater state involvement in the economy. Sustainable development policies could also challenge the way traditional political institutions function, as new forms of private regulation that circumvent state institutions proliferate. Governments are now placing significant emphasis on notions of 'sustainable consumption and production', and commercial efforts to change consumption patterns such as 'ethical shopping' and 'green consumerism' proliferate across the region.

Conclusion

As a rapidly growing region, Latin America offers insights into an aspect of political risk that is growing in importance in the developing world: environmental disputes, which are now posing complex new political and social challenges for foreign investors. Yet political risk insurance globally – a dynamic, growing business – remains dominated by standard forms of coverage that concentrate heavily on issues of violence such as civil unrest and terrorism, the expropriation of assets, the repudiation of contracts and currency fluctuation. It has tended to overlook as a risk factor this growing source of activism in the developing world.

The operational risk posed to organizations by environmental disputes is hard to evaluate in quantitative terms – and even harder to plan for. But as with all responses to political risk, a good understanding of a country, a well-informed awareness of broader socio-political factors that are likely to have a bearing on a project from the outset, and internal processes that incorporate environmental factors within the very fabric of corporate decision making, will give risk managers a head start. Moreover, there is a clear competitive advantage to developing a fuller understanding of the environmental factors that can influence a project: risk assessment is increasingly being seen as a key tool to achieving sustainable development because it requires regulators and businesses to assess the level of risk that can be tolerated against the cost of reducing it. Ultimately, as beneficiaries of the public goods that comprise natural capital, corporations have as much of a stake in safeguarding the environment of the emerging markets in whose territories they operate as the communities that live there. A strategic vision that recognizes this, provides transparency through plausible communication, and makes participation with these stakeholders a central aspiration, is much more likely to succeed.

Notes

1   Center for Climate and Energy Solutions (C2ES) (2013) *Weathering the Storm: Building business resilience to climate change*, Arlington, VA

2   Multilateral Investment Guarantee Agency (MIGA) (2013) *2012 World Investment and Political Risk*, Washington

3   IDB (2012) *The Climate and Development Challenge for Latin America and the Caribbean: Options for climate-resilient, low-carbon development*, Washington

Further reading

ClimateWise (2013) *What could excellence in incorporating low-carbon decision making in insurance and reinsurance investment strategies look like?* ClimateWise/Cambridge Programme for Sustainability Leadership (CPSL), University of Cambridge (www.climatewise.org.uk)

Cranfield University/Defra (2011) *Green Leaves III: Guidelines for environmental risk assessment and management*, Collaborative Centre of Excellence in Understanding and Managing Natural and Environmental Risks, Cranfield University/Department for Environment and Rural Affairs (Defra)

Curtin, Tom (2006), *Managing Green Issues*, Palgrave Macmillan, Basingstoke

Richardson, Bryan and Gerzon, Peter, *Emergent Risks, IRM Research Paper*, Institute of Risk Management (IRM), London

Business risk in Russia: root causes and future trends

CARLO GALLO, ENQUIRISK

Introduction

The ousting of Ukraine's president Viktor Yanukovich and Russia's military intervention in, and subsequent annexation of, Crimea have brought Russia-West relations to their lowest point since Soviet times. As this chapter goes to press on 18 March, the EU and the United States are considering deeper sanctions, after ineffectual travel bans and asset freezes against key Russian individuals. For the first time since the start of the crisis, a Ukrainian soldier has reportedly been shot dead in Crimea.

The extent to which the Russia-West confrontation will escalate is currently highly uncertain. However, even a relatively benign scenario, where Russia and the West manage to avoid the heaviest of sanctions, let alone a military confrontation, would likely deepen a number of pre-existing structural problems of the Russian business environment. This chapter is focused on those structural challenges and how they are likely to interact with a growing chill in relations with the West. However, a discussion of more extreme scenarios, for example the potential for "Iran-style" western sanctions against Russia, is beyond the scope of this chapter.

Even before the diplomatic crisis, doing business in Russia required thorough preparation. Despite some improvement at the margins, as reflected in the improved ranking in the 2014 World Bank *Doing Business* report (see below), business risks remain deeply rooted in Russia's political and economic system. These risks include systemic corruption, administrative pressure, political and regulatory uncertainty, cumbersome red tape and infrastructure bottlenecks. While the risk profile is less worrying than in many other resource-rich emerging markets, the risk/reward ratio associated with investing in Russia has arguably worsened compared to the pre-crisis years.

Are you seeing the full picture?

Political instability. Economic nationalism. Regulatory change. Conflict. Social unrest. Terrorism. Crime. Corruption.

Managing complex political risks requires a vast range of diverse skills, impossible to find in any one organisation.

Our web-based expert network gives you fast, tailored and cost effective access to **specialist insights on a global scale**.

ENQUIRISK

Smart Access To Risk Expertise
www.enquirisk.com

Russian GDP grew by about 1.3 per cent in 2013, and is currently expected to grow by 1 per cent or less in 2014. This is much lower than the 7 per cent averaged in the years before the 2008 economic crisis, and it signals lower average returns on investment. However, business risks have not decreased since then to match that decline. On the contrary, political uncertainty is on the increase. Not only has the economic and political course undertaken by President Vladimir Putin exhausted its potential to sustain growth by now, it has also severely undermined the rule of law, nurtured corruption and fuelled an unsustainable economic and political addition to the oil rent.

Russia's intervention in Ukraine, and its growing confrontation with the West, both reflect and further promote the leadership's reliance on nationalist sentiments, instead of economic performance, as a means to shore up popular support. This will likely weaken the prospects for economic modernisation and structural reforms; it will fuel economic protectionism, boost the role of the state in the economy and further undermine the rule of law.

Business risks in context

In order to gauge the future trajectory of business risks, one needs to go beyond the headlines and gain a deep understanding of 'how Russia works'. The problems often ascribed to the Russian business environment are in fact only the symptoms of more fundamental and structural problems. These structural problems have their roots in the very stubborn legacy of the Soviet system. US economists Clifford Gaddy and Barry Ickes (1999) have shown that, despite the tremendous changes that have occurred elsewhere in the economy, a considerable portion of Russian industry, particularly its machine-building core, remains largely unreformed from its Soviet days and is unfit for market conditions. It escaped reform and restructuring during the 1990s and remains unviable yet vital for the country's political and social stability, as it still accounts for a considerable share of workforce employment. The most extreme cases are those where entire towns depend on just one or two inefficient plants for the bulk of local employment. There are hundreds of such 'mono-towns'. They account for 13–17 per cent of total employment in manufacturing across the country, and for over a third of employment in the industrial Urals region (Commander, Nikoloski and Plekhanov 2011: 15, 27). Within Russian manufacturing, unviable plants are particularly prevalent in the military industry. Most plants in this sector enjoy monopoly status as suppliers of a particular weapon or product and can charge high prices for output generally regarded as low quality.

Oxenstierna and Westerlund (2013) report that in 2012 the defence industrial sector numbered 1,353 companies employing 2 million workers. They found that Russian defence companies tend to have from twice to four times as many employees as Western companies with comparable sales revenues. The problem of low industrial competitiveness and labour productivity is wider than reflected in mono-towns and defence companies.

Putin's version of CSR

Gaddy and Ickes (2013) have explained how Putin propped up and revitalized 'dinosaur industries' starting from 2000, using the rent extracted by natural resource companies at times of rapidly rising oil prices. The redistribution of the resource rent towards unviable heavy industry still occurs to this day, and takes place mostly by informal mechanisms, as opposed to via taxation and state subsidies. The main mechanism of redistribution consists in forcing oil and gas producers, as well as pipelines and transport companies, to provide their goods and services to unviable manufacturers at below market prices, and to purchase their machinery at above market prices.

Both state and private resource and infrastructure companies are involved in the redistribution. Since coming to power in 2000 Putin has in a few years amassed sufficient power to induce private companies to comply with this rent redistribution scheme under threat of state sanctions or even renationalization, a threat whose credibility was visibly demonstrated by the end of 2003 with the Yukos case. Because most oligarchs acquired their assets in dubious ways in the 1990s, and because law enforcement and the courts are subordinated to the executive branch of power, the threat remains credible.

Implications for the business climate

The rent redistribution pattern underscores how social stability, and therefore political stability, are dependent on the ability of the state to keep channelling resources to inefficient enterprises. Moreover, Putin is becoming increasingly reliant on the support of the more state-dependent sections of the electorate for his personal political support, as reflected in his promise of ever-increasing social spending. However, a slowing economy casts serious doubts on the long-term ability of the current economic and political model to keep delivering on its social spending promises.

As suggested by the recent confrontation with the West, the authorities are likely to lean more on nationalist sentiments to shore up popular support, than on an increasingly elusive economic performance. This recalibration in the nature of political legitimation can work quite well for a few years: the more state-dependent strata of the population are also those who tend to harbour the greater suspicion of the West, not least because they are the most receptive to the official propaganda spread by state-controlled national TV channels.

Administrative pressure

The rent redistribution model also has more direct implications for foreign investors that operate in the sectors directly involved in the redistribution: they are formally or informally expected to comply with its demands. This is clearly seen in the electricity generation sector, which has attracted considerable foreign investment in recent years and has been hailed as an example of successful privatization. In fact, the government keeps capping the electricity prices, which will remain frozen in 2014, thus severely undermining the ability of foreign companies to run their business effectively.

The recent deepening of confrontation with the West will probably further reduce the incentives for structural economic reforms, including privatizations. However, even in the unlikely event that they are implemented to such an extent as to significantly reduce state ownership in key sectors, they are not necessarily going to introduce market efficiency. Indeed, the firms operating in the sectors involved in the rent redistribution scheme (extractive and infrastructure industries first of all) will remain severely constrained in their basic business decisions. Putin's approach to state–business relations gives a whole new meaning to such terms as 'state capitalism' and 'corporate social responsibility'.

The risk that foreign investors will face unfair competition and administrative pressure to conform with the rent redistribution model is less prominent in sectors where the Soviet economy did not produce large dinosaurs: food and consumer retail, IT and telecommunications, tourism, light industry etc. However, the growing risk of international diplomatic and economic isolation also increases the risk of formal and informal discrimination against western investors in all sectors. Moreover, even without assuming international isolation, the opacity of the political and economic model affects the whole economy by sustaining corruption, conflict of interests within government and regulatory bodies, and a weak rule of law.

Resistance to political and economic modernization

Because the rent redistribution mechanisms are largely informal (effectively mandated by the state under a veiled threat), they reinforce Putin's ability to adopt a highly informal, centralized and personalistic method of political rule in other spheres too. This involves relying on patronage and personal loyalties, instead of institutions, to run the country and provides fertile ground for systemic corruption and regulatory volatility.

The ruling circle needs politics to remain informal and institutions to remain weak because institutions can potentially be captured by opponents. Under the current set-up, Putin can remain in charge even when moving from the presidency to the post of prime minister, as he did in 2008–2012. If power resided with the institution, instead of with the person, whoever held the presidency would rule instead.

The rent redistribution model and the fact that state salaries have increased over Putin's terms help explain the support of large portions of the Russian electorate for Putin, who see him as the most credible guarantor of a paternalistic style of economic management. Most Russians live in medium and small cities and their living standards strongly depend on state assistance, salaries or pensions (eg teachers, doctors, military and police personnel, local administration officials).

This creates a powerful constituency against genuine economic reform. State-dependent voters are suspicious of liberal and pro-market slogans, as they rightly fear that they imply a less paternalistic economic course. So, if the political system became more institutionalized and democratic, they would likely use new opportunities for political participation in order to promote even greater populism and hamper economic modernization.

Strengthening democratic institutions, the rule of law and market mechanisms would be necessary in order to modernize the economy, improve its competitiveness and attract badly needed foreign technology and capital. However, militating against the realization of such scenarios is not only the self-interests of the narrow ruling elite, for which democratization carries the risk of losing power (and probably of coming under investigation too), but also the fact that the bulk of Russian voters would use the new democratic rights to vote against economic modernization.

It is quite clear that the sizeable but inefficient sections of the Russian economy are bound to suffer from a path of growing international economic integration. The rift with the West, by potentially triggering a regression to isolationism and/or closer relations with non-Western state capitalist economies, would likely facilitate the survival of the rent redistribution economic model. Putin's Eurasian Union *regional* integration project is likely supposed to help preserve this economic model as long as possible, among other motivations.

Trends in business risks

Despite a growing risk of general economic isolation, the Russian investment landscape will likely remain very diverse and risks will continue to vary widely depending on the sector of operation, the attitude of the regional administration, the background and agenda of local business partners, as well as the investor's entry strategies and operational choices on the ground. Risks can be managed and mitigated. Indeed, growing risk perceptions associated with deteriorating relations with the West can turn into growing opportunities for those who know how to navigate the Russian business environment.

Large multinationals tend to have better recourse against local-level corruption risks, such as bribe demands connected with local business permits and audits, than SMEs. In general, local manufacturing tends to carry significantly more risks than import/export operations. Sectors where local competitors have direct or indirect connections with top political or law enforcement players often carry significant risk of administrative pressure and unfair competition.

In connection with strategic investments, it is important to map the preferences of key political groupings in order to forecast the likely direction of regulatory policy for any given sector of the economy. In particular, investors need to understand the attitudes of senior members of the political and business elites towards foreign investment in that area. This can be done effectively by researching the formal and informal links that exist between major political players and local businesses with which investors may be interacting, such as partners, suppliers or competitors.

In the first part of this chapter, I suggested that business risks have much deeper roots than are often acknowledged by the authorities or by investors themselves. As such, they are much more difficult to overcome. Moreover, if worsening relations with the West lead to a retrenchment from the global economy and greater protectionism, this will likely support the rent redistribution model for a few years at least.

However, this would in turn accelerate economy deterioration. How long will the government keep postponing the day of reckoning? Will it wait until economic reforms will be more socially painful, unmanageable and unpredictable? Below is a quick glance at developments and trends in key business risk areas, to gauge the extent of government commitment to genuine political and economic modernization.

Privatizations

Official estimates indicate that roughly 50 per cent of the Russian economy is under state control. The government plans to decrease that share substantially by 2020, and possibly to 25 per cent. In practice, however, the latest privatization plans are confined to the sale of minority stakes in such state companies as oil transportation company Transneft, power generation company RusHydro, oil and gas companies Rosneft, Zarubezhneft, rail transport company RZhD and bank VTB. The government has several times delayed the implementation of privatizations citing difficult market conditions.

In any case, the Law on Strategic Sectors of 2008 restricts the ability of foreign investors to acquire stakes in Russian companies operating in 42 sectors. Moreover, as discussed above, private ownership does not necessarily translate into freedom to operate according to commercial or market principles, as formal and informal administrative pressure tends to affect companies that operate within the areas of the rent redistribution model.

Corruption

Transparency International's 2013 Perceptions of Corruption Index ranked Russia as 127th out of 177 surveyed countries (where the least corrupt country is ranked first). For comparison, Brazil and South Africa both ranked 72nd, China 80th, and India 94th. Russia's dismal record is ultimately a function of its weak legal institutions and informal political rule. Democratic controlling institutions have been emasculated or eliminated during Putin's terms and the trend continues.

Corruption remains rampant at all levels of public officialdom, but particularly where large state contracts are at stake. Russia's chief military prosecutor, Sergei Fridinsky, estimated that 20 per cent of the defence budget is stolen every year. This is likely a conservative estimate, as independent observers put it at up to 50 per cent. It is worth adding that the government is due to spend 19,000 billion roubles (about $630 billion) in arms procurement over 2011–2020. Similarly, on 9 January 2014, Gian-Franco Kasper, a Swiss member of the International Olympic Committee said that about a third of the $55 billion spent on the 2014 Sochi Winter Olympics had been stolen due to corruption.

A sign of the government's lacking commitment in the fight against corruption so far has been its failure to ratify Article 20 of the UN Convention against Corruption, which Russia signed in 2003. The article establishes criminal responsibility for public officials having income or assets whose origin they cannot explain. A bill for the ratification of this article was introduced to parliament in February 2013, but its fate remains uncertain.

Finally, in October 2013 Putin introduced a constitutional amendment bill to merge the Arbitrage Court with the Supreme Court. The initiative is a direct blow against the Arbitrage Court, which is widely seen as the most impartial part of the Russian court system and would effectively be liquidated with the amendment.

Technological modernization

In October 2013 Putin acknowledged that Russia's labour productivity is too low at 3.1 per cent, which is less than half the level of most developed economies. Putin pledged to increase it 'in the coming years' to 5–6 per cent a year. However Putin has promised similar improvements several times in the past and progress has been slow. Low labour productivity is a symptom of the inefficiency of Russian industry. In Putin's mind, modernization effectively means equipping existing plants with new technology and better management, but without drastic restructuring (and the related loss of jobs). Technology transfer is indeed happening in some key areas of Russian manufacturing, such as with international joint ventures or major acquisitions in the automotive and defence sectors.

But a large programme of procurement of foreign equipment, while stimulating the technological modernization of inefficient domestic plants, also undermines the logic of the rent redistribution model, which compels profitable companies to buy the output (mostly machinery) of inefficient plants. For example, the famous Russian Sukhoi fighter jet has been produced in recent years with the input of a great deal of foreign technology and components (Hanson, 2011:9). However, in January 2014 the government restricted the import of foreign equipment for Russia's defence sector in order to incentivize the purchase of local equipment instead. The restriction applies to all cases where a Russian-made 'equivalent product' exists, and the Ministry of Industry and Trade will decide, apparently on a case-by-case basis, if a locally-produced product exists. This highlights the continued attempt by the government to enforce the rent redistribution model by dictating economic decisions to enterprises from above.

Administrative barriers to doing business

Russia's ranking in the World Bank's *Doing Business* report improved from 111th to 92th between the 2013 and the latest (2014) editions. The greatest improvement was recorded in the administrative process businesses need to go through in order to get connected to the electricity grid. However, the number of days that typically elapse before a business is connected (162) and the cost of doing so (294 per cent of income per capita) are still significantly higher than the OECD average (89 and 79 per cent). In early 2012 Putin tasked the government to achieve a ranking of 50th by 2015 and 20th by 2018. These appear to be very ambitious targets. In any case, these targets will help the government focus on measurable improvements in the selected areas covered by the index. However, the index does not reflect other vitally important aspects of the business environment, such as the level of corruption and the independence of the courts etc.

Political reform

About 60 per cent of Russians mistrust the authorities, believing that they are corrupt, ineffective, unfair and self-interested. Yet, for all the corruption and, increasingly, the economic stagnation associated with the political and economic system built by Vladimir Putin, the impetus for change from below is very feeble. Putin's military intervention in Crimea has pushed his approval ratings toward record historical levels. Even the educated middle classes, who tend to be more likely to support pro-democratic change, appear to "rally under the flag" of Putin's military assertiveness. As explained above, pro-Putin sentiments among the state-dependent, paternalist layers of the population are even stronger. This would likely change only if their socio-economic conditions were to deteriorate sharply.

This could occur if oil prices were to fall stably under $70–80 per barrel for two or more years. Even then, the kind of change these groups would demand is unlikely to be pro-market and liberal. To avert social discontent among his core supporters, Putin has boosted social spending significantly in the last few years. Over a trillion roubles ($30bn) is spent yearly to balance the pension fund. Pension reform, such as increasing the pension age, has been postponed numerous times, while Putin has issued promises and decrees mandating higher social spending. These plans are increasingly impossible to fulfil and have already contributed to a worrying increase in public debt at the level of regional governments, from $35 billion in 2010 to an estimated $78 billion in 2014.

Putin and his close circle of associates have been trying to find a balance between preserving their control over political and economic power on the one hand, and trying to improve the quality of governance on the other. Nationalism and a more assertive stance towards the West could provide a third way. For years Putin appeared unable to find a consistent strategy for economic modernization, rather oscillating between tentative liberalization and authoritarian regression. Since 2012, he appears to have taken a more decisive turn towards the authoritarian model, likely to be increasingly buttressed by nationalism.

Conclusion

Putin's model of state-directed and oil-fuelled capitalism had already exhausted its ability to deliver growth before his military intervention in, and annexation of, Crimea. The ensuing diplomatic conflict with the West is likely to provide a boost to his popularity, and to divert attention from structural economic problems, at least for one or two years. The fact remains, however, that the government lacks a credible and coherent strategy for managing the change and promoting economic and political modernization. By stalling and buying time, Russia will face the risk of declining oil prices, reducing its ability to spend its way out of instability. There is a credible risk that protest sentiments will eventually increase, though large-scale unrest is unlikely in the next few years. Confrontation with the West will probably help Putin minimize the risk of elite divisions and of the emergence of an organized opposition. Eventually, however, a reduced oil pie and Putin's weakening ability to deliver political stability and economic growth will likely intensify intra-elite jostling.

The current trend for rapidly deteriorating relations with the West requires companies to be even more vigilant than ever, in order to decipher the potential impact of western economic sanctions and Russian reaction. Choosing the appropriate investment strategy and strategic partners is more important than ever. Political risk is on the rise, but can be effectively mitigated and managed to achieve commercial success if companies place risk management at the centre of their Russia strategies. After all, Russia remains a vast consumer market and one of the most compelling investment cases globally in the extractive sectors.

References

Commander, S, Nikoloski, Z and Plekhanov, A (2011) *Employment concentration and resource allocation: One-company towns in Russia.* Working Paper, Discussion Paper series, Forschungsinstitut zur Zukunft der Arbeit, No 6034

Gaddy, C G and Ickes, B W (2013) *Prosperity in Depth: Russia – caught in the bear trap,* The Legatum Institute, London

Gaddy, C G and Ickes, B W (1999) *Russia's Virtual Economy,* Brookings Institution

Hanson, P (2011) *Risks in Russia – is the environment changing?* Tartu School of Economics, Electronic Publications of Pan-European Institute, no 6, Tartu

Oxenstierna, S and Westerlund, F (2013) 'Arms procurement and the Russian defense industry: challenges up to 2020', *Journal of Slavic Military Studies,* **26**, pp 1–24

Sustainability risk management in China

JAMES M PEARSON, PACIFIC RISK ADVISORS

Introduction

In this chapter we update and further explore how sustainability risk management and related issues are being addressed and considered in China. We are looking to analyse the implications of these risks to potential investors and those already in China. In updating and developing this chapter we have also explored the new and existing drivers for change both internally within China and externally on the investors.

Over the last few years there has been an enormous increase in the awareness and understanding of sustainability-related issues by institutions, corporations and the public alike. The 12th Five-Year Plan (FYP) (2011–15) is now in its 3rd year of implementation where China is trying to re-orientate its policy from maximizing growth to balancing growth with social harmony and environmental sustainability. This reorientation has created many challenges in changing mindsets at state, company and public level. Efforts in establishing low-carbon regulations and emissions trading platforms, encouraging growth of environmental industries and managing public concerns, has taken a lot more effort than envisaged. These changes have resulted in raised levels of concern, and a number of public demonstrations. As a greater understanding is realized of the current state of the environment, the risks and the resources needed to manage them is apparent. At the end of 2013 significant air pollution episodes have occurred throughout the country and especially in Beijing. Media are now speculating that the environmental degradation is so severe, with such stark domestic and international repercussions, that pollution poses not only a major long-term burden on the Chinese public but also an acute political challenge to the ruling Communist Party.

The head of China's top economic planning agency told the parliament in December 2013 that the country is not even halfway to meeting its environmental targets for 2015 set out in the FYP. This does not bode well for the remainder of the FYP and overall environmental performance in China.

PACIFIC RISK
A d v i s o r s

We identify sustainability-related opportunitiesand risks throughout the lifetime of an investment.

Our focus is to create and implement sustainable value at both strategic and operational levels.

We advise on environmental, health, safety and social issues faced by investors and operators in Asia.

For further details on how we can assist you, contact:

James Pearson – CEO

20F Central Tower 28 Queens Road Central Hong Kong

james.pearson@pacificriskadvisors.com

Tel: +852 8199 0535

www.pacificriskadvisors.com

These risks have generated significant interest about the potential opportunities for business and growth as new environmental and sustainability-related industries emerge. Significant opportunities have been created but there have been difficulties in capturing and generating the values as the boundaries shift. For instance the solar panel industry has seen enormous shifts in fortunes and consolidation. Even so a recent McKinsey report estimates that for every five-year period over the next 20 years, China could achieve a 17–18 per cent reduction on energy intensity per GDP unit. However this level could still require China to rely on importing up to 80 per cent of its coal and oil requirements.

It is recognized that these issues are not historically linked to private consumption as in the West; but they are linked to the enormous growth and industrial processes that China's economy relies on. In the past, China has not seen the pollution issue as an immediate problem, since economic growth is still the priority. The largest drivers for change are not from external parties or concern about the planet; rather, they are initiatives as a result of increasing health and economic implications and costs within the country. It is currently estimated that 1 per cent of the 560 million city dwellers breathe air considered safe by the European Union. Healthcare and other indirect costs are major concerns for the Party and planners going forward.

We attempt to explore some of these risks and opportunities in this chapter and discuss key elements in successfully managing a sustainability risk strategy as an investor. To enable investors to maximize their opportunities despite changes in the macro environment, we touch on a major shift in the management of these risks through establishing post-investment and pre-exit strategies. Hence capturing the 'sustainable value' that enhanced environmental and social management can have on an investment.

Significant financial investment, regulatory implementation and cultural change are required to solve the problems inherent in social development, such as technological innovation, educational development, pollution control and ecological improvement. These investments are being made, but time and the rate of change are critical factors.

Setting the scene

Sustainability risks and issues are becoming firmly integrated into our normal business and day-to-day life, and sustainability is no longer a stranger to the boardroom discussion. Throughout this chapter we have used the term 'sustainability' to encompass a wide range of considerations that include environmental, health, safety, energy and climate, labour, and social responsibility. Other relevant terms commonly used are:

- Corporate social responsibility (CSR) is mainly focused on the working community, labour and social issues and charity functions.
- Environmental social governance (ESG) and socially responsible investment (SRI) are oriented to the financial sector where ESG status and performance are key elements in determining whether a potential investment presents appropriately manageable sustainability-related risks.

- International Finance Corporation (IFC) Performance Standards are a series of eight integrated defined responsibilities for investors managing their environmental and social risks. Required for all IFC-related clients, but many institutions use these as benchmarks in the absence of any similar local guidance.
- IFC Guidance Notes are companion documents to the performance standards, providing guidance in meeting the performance standards.
- The Equator Principles, which have been adopted by many financial institutions, are a means by which projects are developed in a manner that is socially responsible and reflect sound environmental management practices.
- Under the United Nations Principles for Responsible Investment (UNPRI) investors have agreed to a duty to act in the best long-term interests of their beneficiaries. In this role, ESG issues can affect the performance of investment portfolios and better align investors with the broader objectives of society.

As can be seen from the examples above, significant resources have been applied to understanding and managing these issues in a wide variety of industries.

Where are we now?

So how are these issues currently being managed, how are they developing in China and what risks do they represent to current and future investments?

Sustainability and environmental awareness in China is rapidly developing, and there has been a noticeable change in appreciation of the issues, but there is still great opportunity for on-the-ground implementation. Regulators are now starting to tackle the issues at factories proactively and not just wait for a complaint to be made or identified by third-party audits. But the culture of governmental control still means that corporations are often not taking on and managing their own sustainability responsibilities. This is now more than ever to their detriment as opportunities can be missed. These can include government subsidies and funding, use of more efficient technologies and alternative energy sources.

Major threats to the environment

In Dec 2013, the Chinese government announced that about 3.33 million hectares of farmland in China is too polluted for growing crops.

In 2012, the MEP (Ministry for Environmental Protection) admitted that water and air pollution have received the most attention from the Chinese government. The 2012 Environmental Conditions Report states that 57.3 per cent of the groundwater in 198 cities in 2012 was 'bad' or 'extremely bad', whilst over 30 per cent of the country's major rivers were 'polluted' or 'seriously polluted'.

Only 27 out of 113 key cities met overall air quality standards in 2012.

A survey conducted by the Economist Intelligence Unit (2008) indicated that sustainability and environment risk is not considered as part of the main risk management agenda, that overall responsibility of these issues is a significant grey area, and that there are no clear lines of responsibility and accountability. This is still seen as the case, but light is slowly emerging at the end of the tunnel. Understanding of these issues, and a willingness to address them, needs to be further nurtured within senior management levels so that performance can be improved. With the increase in opportunities in the environmental industry market, and the indirect benefits to many industries, senior management levels are rapidly appreciating the options open to them.

A key area of concern remains the transparency within the supply chain and ultimately the reputational risk exposure of the key stakeholders, especially within the manufacturing sector. This market area is a significant element of China's GDP and there are enormous efforts being made to address these concerns through contractual means, third-party assessments, partnering and education. Investors and stakeholders are now seeking greater visibility of not just their own activities but those of their partners and suppliers abroad.

This has been particularly brought to mind with the recent Bangladesh Tazreen Factory Fire (November 2012) where 112 people died and the Rana Plaza factory collapse in April 2013 that killed 1,100 people. Many multinationals were indirectly associated with these premises and major changes to the industry have been implemented. For example, Li & Fung announced in January 2014 the creation of a new business unit to focus more intensely on factory and worker safety following the recent tragedies in the garment industry. The Group Chairman, Dr William K Fung, is leading the initiative and it will be an integral part of Li & Fung's new three-year business plan. Initiatives such as these will have an impact on companies with a large manufacturing vendor base in China.

This high-level corporate commitment is an indication of how much these sustainability-related risks are being part and parcel of the board's agenda and concerns.

Whilst assessing potential ESG liabilities prior to an investment has also become far more common over the last 10 years, there are still many investors who do not formally consider these liabilities as part of the transaction. Contamination and liability-related regulations are developing as the costs associated with clean-up, clean air and providing potable water are being realized. These risks are being compounded with the advent of new regulations and improved enforcement of existing regulations. Tie this in with the lack of appreciation of supply chain risk and some investors will be getting their fingers burnt.

There are also increasing pressures on direct investors (ie private equity funds), not only identifying their risks pre-investment, but also managing and reporting on these risks during the post-investment period. These pressures are coming from limited partners (LPs), especially large institutional investors who in turn are being charged with reporting on ESG performance for all their funds. These pressures are also being replicated by stakeholders and other shareholders in public equities where ESG performance is becoming a standard reporting metric. The more advanced funds are looking at how to capture sustainable value within their portfolios, whilst the less advanced are just getting to grips with the implications of ESG.

The lack of transparency in many company operations is a main concern for external investors, and the result of a lack of internal communication in response to the pressures from LPs and stakeholders etc. Without an appropriate communication system in place, investors cannot be sure that information relating to sustainability risks is being fully passed on to them. Concern not only lies in the transparency, but also in the board's capability in understanding the implications of these risks to the businesses they are running.

There remains little public information on engagement practices between investors and companies in China on ESG issues. Obtaining ESG data can be frustrating as many investor relations staff do not understand ESG and confuse it with charitable giving.

There has also been a significant increase over the last 10 years in the need to identify environmental liabilities and meet specific environmental criteria (IFC PS, Equator Principles, UNPRI etc) as a requirement of bank lending. Consideration is also being extended to market expectations and sustainability reporting requirements at exit and how these issues can be addressed over the life of an investment. Use of post-investment ESG management and reporting mechanisms can be part of the overall investment approach to capturing ESG values.

Stock exchanges have also been concerned about ESG risks for new and existing listings and many such as Taiwan, Malaysia, Hong Kong and Shanghai have implemented reporting requirements. Integrating this with the growth of ESG indices and research groups and the increasing need to use ESG as a market differentiator is another driving factor for making the boardroom more aware of the opportunities in ESG.

Regulatory enforcement

For an emerging market, the environmental legislation in China is progressive; however, implementation of environmental legislation varies widely across the country. To summarize the main requirements in regulatory approaches:

- *Centralized pollution control*: State Council and MEP issued documents requiring central and regional governments to promote centralized control of waste within their jurisdictions.

- *Environmental impact assessment (EIA)*: an EIA is required for every project with a potential negative environmental impact. Approval by the national or regional environmental administration is required before a project can be formally launched.

- *'Three synchronies' system*: this requires that the design, construction and operation of a new industrial project must be synchronized with the design, construction and operation of appropriate pollution treatment facilities.

- *Emission/discharge quality standards*: these require compliance with discharge and ambient standards to help the move from concentration-based to mass-based or total pollution load control.

- *Discharge permit system*: permits are issued that limit both the quantities and concentrations of pollutants in wastewater and air emissions.
- *Pollution control*: reduction of waste releases. Clean-up deadlines imposed by national or local governments with the risk of being fined or shut down.

Environmental performance

Recent incidents that attracted considerable international media attention, such as smog across Chinese cities and the large-scale dead pigs scandal in Huangpu River have prompted more focus on performance:

- in 2013, Shandong Provincial MEP offered RMB100,000 (£9,700) for information regarding factories breaking waste disposal rules;

- in May 2013, the MEP suspended 15 factories breaking air/water pollution laws;

- in August 2013, the MEP received 140 complaints through its hotline resulting in 10 plants being shut down and others subject to immediate corrective actions, suspension or fines;

- the reduction targets in the FYP are 8 per cent chemical oxygen demand (COD) and sulfur dioxide (SO_2), and 10 per cent ammonia nitrogen and nitrogen oxides (NOx) compared with 2010 levels;

- in 2011, the MEP organized a national drill on environmental emergency response, the scenario being a large-scale chemical spill near a drinking water source.

Sustainability risks and opportunities

It is often the case that senior management are struggling to understand and come to terms with the rapid pace of change and demands placed on them by business-related sustainability expectations. Some issues are obviously easier to comprehend, such as separation of wastes, which allows a better price to be obtained. However, the wider implications of soil and groundwater contamination and associated costs for clean-up, indirect health costs paid for by the state or suppliers cutting corners, are often seen to be outside a management purview. The realization that past waste disposal practices or poor occupational exposure management, or even one of its suppliers' poor operations, can come back to haunt the performance of a company is a difficult pill to swallow. Additional sustainability-related risks being faced are:

- *Reputational threats* caused by the failure of companies to address their own environmental, safety or social impacts. Poor environmental, health, safety and labour issues have resulted in reputational damage to companies that fail to change their practices to reduce their impact on the environment.

- *Fire and life safety disasters* that could have been avoided seriously damage the reputation of industries as a whole, such as the poultry processing factory fire in June 2013 that killed 120 people.

- *Product and food safety threats* have been realized through scandals involving milk contamination, lead paint in toys, skin whitening cream and phthalates in plastic toys. In May 2013, Guangdong Province officials stated they had discovered excessive levels of cadmium in 155 batches of rice collected from markets, restaurants and storehouses. Of those, 89 were from Hunan Province. In December 2013 a vice-minister of land and resources, Wang Shiyuan, said that 8 million acres of China's farmland had become so polluted that planting crops on it 'should not be allowed'.

- *Market regulation grey areas* have allowed poor practices to thrive such as allowing dead pigs to enter the food chain. A clampdown resulted in the dead pigs being thrown into the Huangpu River, rather than into disposal pits, causing major water quality concerns.

- *New taxes, new compliance measures and new legislation* concerning the fight against climate change are being implemented. Significant changes in energy policy and energy efficiency regulations are impacting all areas. For some companies these will turn profitable enterprises into unprofitable ones virtually overnight.

- *Environmental performance and lending are being linked* and Chinese banks are now in a position to include previous environmental fines and citations in their decision criteria regarding loans and financing. Tying this in with international bank criteria such as the IFC PS, Equator Principles and UNPRI, companies with poor sustainability records will be finding it harder and more expensive to borrow.

- *Directors' liability* is increasingly important as liabilities for global operations are coming back to haunt the boardroom. Changes in regulations in Australia, the United Kingdom and the United States are exposing directors to far greater personal liability for the sustainability performance of their operations.

- *The new Chinese Labour Law* has raised many concerns among factory owners through reduced working hours and higher pay. Chinese authorities have been active in blacklisting many local and multinational companies that have not been compliant.

- *Stakeholder and community actions* have seen significant increases in community activity against developments, industrial expansions, land grabbing and resettlement, reflecting a far greater need for liaison and community consultation and engagement.

Raising the issue of strategic sustainability planning for a business that encompasses environmental risks, CSR and ESG principles and integrates with the existing risk management strategy is often but not always met with incomprehension. However, we are seeing an increase in understanding the importance of these issues at management and executive levels as the risks are becoming more apparent and can be related to their own spheres of influence. The opportunity for establishing an integrated Business Continuity Planning process to package these risks is becoming a valuable approach. With the increase in understanding and realization, new business opportunities, approaches and technologies are being identified to create a 'sustainability industry' and market. This is helping companies to find a niche market and using sustainability approaches as a market differentiator.

These opportunities have also stimulated an enormous rise in the number of funds and investments in China related to climate change, carbon, renewable energy, clean technologies, pollution control, waste management and recycling and conservation. These have been enhanced by innovative funding arrangements, the resurrection of performance-based contracts supported by government guarantees and environmental finance initiatives. These developments open the door to many new opportunities and markets that have previously been dormant or just not recognized.

The State Council has recognized this and in August 2013 announced plans to make the energy-saving sector a 'pillar' of the economy by 2015. The environmental protection sector is predicted to increase by 15 per cent on average annually, reaching an output of RMB4.5 trillion (£474 billion).

Conclusions

We can conclude the following from the current market potential for sustainable related businesses, the opportunities for change and the influence of variable world markets. The financial crisis, whilst slowing investments down, has not dulled the need for or interest in environmental industry opportunities. If anything, it has further stimulated the need to review all operations and approaches to optimize performance.

The Chinese environmental market holds out enormous opportunities for foreign companies. There has already been significant investment in environmental technology and this will continue over the next 20 years. The opportunities lie in technologies and provision of expertise and capital.

Investment will be driven mainly by economic necessity to maintain the planned growth, but increasingly also by the realization that in the long term the Chinese economy will benefit only from sustainable growth.

Sustainability risk management is an important business issue that is quickly becoming a mandatory requirement. Unlike other business issues, sustainability issues are being shaped by drivers outside an individual industry's control. Numerous Chinese and non-Chinese stakeholders are demanding that companies address it, ensuring that it will be in the spotlight for many years.

Investors' approach to sustainability issues should be disciplined and structured. This means that procedures should be put in place to strategically align and evaluate the operational implications of sustainability strategies, drive collaboration across the supply chain, and develop governance and control structures that both guide and measure progress.

There are compelling financial, regulatory, risk mitigation and broader market opportunities for the inclusion of sustainability strategies within business models.

Directors' liability is increasingly a key driver for companies to understand and manage their sustainability risks in an international market.

Companies are going to have to engage in sustainability management if they are not to be caught out by the many challenges facing them in a world where information is easily accessible. This is not just a Western problem, it is a global problem. Involvement of stakeholders, transparency, governance and accountability are key elements in a successful business.

The road towards sustainability risk management and building on the opportunities is long and varied. Many people are starting to see the path but many others still need convincing. As financial markets adjust and more momentum is added we are confident that the opportunities will be realized, the markets captured and that sustainability risk management will become fully integrated into normal business operations.

Further reading

'12 heavy polluters punished under new "green credit" policy', chinadaily.com.cn, 16 November 2007

As China Roars, Pollution Reaches Deadly Extremes, *The New York Times* [online] http://www.nytimes.com/2007/08/26/world/asia/26china.html

China far from Meeting Environmental Targets, *The Wall Street Journal* [online] http://blogs.wsj.com/chinarealtime/2013/12/26/china-far-from-meeting-environmental-targets/

'China's Environmental Blacklist: Shining the light on international companies that haven't heard China's gone green', seedmagazine.com, 13 April 2008

'China's environmental retreat – in tough economic times, promises fall by wayside', washingtonpost.com, 19 November 2008

China to invest in energy saving industries to tackle pollution, *The Euardian* [online] http://www.theguardian.com/environment/chinas-choice/2013/aug/14/china-investment-energy-saving-pollution

Diesendorf, M, *Sustainable Development in China*, sustainabilitycentre.com.au, January 2003

The East is Grey, *The Economist* [online] http://www.economist.com/news/briefing/21583245-china-worlds-worst-polluter-largest-investor-green-energy-its-rise-will-have

Environmental sector China: From major building site to growth market, Deutsche Bank Research, 28 February 2006

The 'Equator Principles': A financial industry benchmark for determining, assessing and managing social and environmental risk in project financing, www.equator-principles.com, November 2005

'Factories Urged to Protect Nature', *China Daily*, 28 February 2006

Honour, D, *Will climate change mitigation see the convergence of business continuity and business sustainability planning?* www.continuitycentral.com, 11 September 2006

KPMG, *China's 12th Five-Year Plan: Sustainability*, April 2011

Lei Zhang and Lijin Zhong, *Integrating environmental risk into China's risk management discourse*, chinaenvironmentallaw.com

Ma Jun, Christine Loh, Wang Jing Jing and Wu Wei, *Hong Kong's Roles in Mending the Disclose Gap*, March 2010

Mak, Liz, 'Taiwan adds social responsibility disclosure to listing rules', 18 December 2008 *21st Century Business Herald* on 19 December 2008, http://chinadigitaltimes.net/china/21st-century-business-herald/?view=all

Mingchun Sun, China: 'Unscathed through the Global Financial Tsunami', *China and World Economy*, vol 17, issue 6, November 2009

OECD, *China in the Global Economy: Government in China*, Chapter 17 'Environment and Governance in China', http://www.keepeek.com/Digital-Asset-Management/oecd/governance/governance-in-china_9789264008441-en#page6

'Polluters Ignore Environmental Laws', *China Daily*, 7 December 2004

The Principles for Responsible Investment, www.unpri.org, January 2006

'Scientific outlook on development', www.chinadaily.com.cn, 12 October 2007

SEPA 'China to require environmental checks for some fund-raising', www.chinaview.cn, 25 February 2008

Siddy, D, Delsus Limited, *Exchanges and sustainable investment*, a report prepared for the World Federation of Exchanges, August 2009

Under the spotlight – the transition of environmental risk management, The Economist Intelligence Unit, 2008

Winds of Change for China's Environment Protection, Ministry of Environmental Protection, People's Republic of China, 15 August 2008

Business risk: developing a marketing and sales strategy for South-East Asia

4.4

STEPHEN GILL, STEPHEN GILL ASSOCIATES

South-East Asia is a sub-region of Asia, consisting of the countries that are geographically south of China, east of India and north of Australia. It is one of the world's most promising and dynamic economic regions in the world and, as such, is high on the priority list of geographical areas for businesses wanting to expand their activities.

The countries that make up South-East Asia are also usually grouped together in international business terms with many multinational companies treating the geographical region as a business region with, perhaps, a head office in one of the major cities such as Singapore, and sub-offices (or country offices) located in a number of the other countries. However, the complexity and diversity of the region presents anyone doing business here with as diverse a set of challenges as they will find anywhere in the world. This chapter looks at the common business practice of developing a marketing/sales strategy for the entire South-East Asia business territory, the risks associated with it, and two commonly used matrix tools that may be used as part of the planning process and that can reduce unforeseen risk.

Marketing and sales are both activities aimed at increasing revenue. They are so closely intertwined that many managers still confuse the two and don't appreciate the differences between them. Indeed, in small organizations, the same people typically perform both sales and marketing tasks. Nevertheless, marketing is different from sales and as the organization grows, the roles and responsibilities become more specialized. We will briefly consider the differences later but first an introduction to South-East Asia.

Geography and population

The region can be divided into two distinct areas. Mainland South-East Asia includes Cambodia, Laos, Myanmar (Burma), Thailand, Vietnam and Peninsular Malaysia. The island (or maritime) nations include East Malaysia, Brunei, Indonesia, the Philippines (which is made up of more than 7,000 islands), Singapore, and East Timor.

South-East Asia has a land area of approximately 4.5 million sq km (1.8 million sq miles) which, putting it into perspective, is about half the size of China and 18 times the size of Great Britain.

The region's combined population is close to 600 million which, in round terms, is double that of the United States, and just over half that of India. The Indonesian island of Java is the most densely populated large island in the world, with Indonesia itself being the most densely populated country. The metropolitan areas of Jakarta, Manila and Bangkok each have populations in excess of 10 million people, and are continuing to grow.

South-East Asia's economics

The region's economy greatly depends upon agriculture, with manufacturing, tourism and services also being important. Indonesia, as an emerging market, is now the largest economy in the region. Singapore and Brunei are established affluent developed economies, with the newly industrialized countries including Malaysia, Thailand and the Philippines. With the exception of Vietnam which is making notably steady progress in developing its industrial sectors, the rest of South-East Asia is still heavily dependent on agriculture and, to some degree, tourism.

Stock markets in South-East Asia have performed better than others in the Asia-Pacific region during recent times but began showing signs of stress as it became clear that South-East Asia could not simply forge ahead irrespective of the tough global conditions. While many national economies continue to post impressive growth, cracks have begun to emerge in the South-East Asian boom, presenting a more uncertain outlook than a year ago.

Political landscape

Although there is no single political voice for the region, the Association of South-East Asian Nations (ASEAN) is an economic and geopolitical organization of 10 countries (Indonesia, Malaysia, the Philippines, Singapore, Thailand, Brunei, Burma (Myanmar), Cambodia, Laos and Vietnam) with aims which include the acceleration of economic growth, social progress, cultural development among its members, the protection of the peace and stability of the region and providing opportunities for member countries to discuss differences peacefully.

Although the region is mainly focused on economics, there have been pockets of political tension such as the anti-government demonstrations in Bangkok. In

Myanmar (Burma) elections appear to have provided a watershed in the country's challenging political landscape. The last 12 months have seen its government embark on a wide-ranging programme of economic and political reforms, prompting the first visit by a US secretary of state in more than 50 years.

Social, cultural and spiritual diversity

The social, cultural and spiritual diversity of South-East Asia is as rich and varied as other aspects of the region. All major religions are represented and also many lesser known ones. Indonesia is the world's largest Muslim nation, and the Philippines is Asia's largest Christian country, while the northern areas are predominately Buddhist.

The region is home to hundreds of languages and peoples that suffer vast inequalities of wealth. The countries' governments range from democracy through to a military dictatorship and various forms of monarchy. The legal systems vary and include Islamic law.

Business marketing/sales strategy and risk

A common marketing/sales strategy for the region, while convenient in business terms, is difficult to achieve in practice due to the sheer size, disparity and diversity of South-East Asia. The alternative, more localized approach to the region which takes account of the varying conditions in each country is far more sensible but may be difficult to manage, particularly if controlled from a central hub. The pros and cons of each approach are not discussed in depth here, as so many business factors influence the choice of strategy; however, some of the common risks involved are highlighted. The range and scope of the risks faced by organizations operating throughout South-East Asia is immense as one may appreciate from the brief introduction to the region given here but that doesn't prevent many of them operating successfully.

Sales vs marketing activities: is there a difference?

The differences between marketing and sales have been debated for years. For the ease of differentiating the two roles here, a simplistic description of them will have to suffice:

- Marketing activities include consumer research (to identify the needs of the customers) and advertising the products/services to raise awareness and build the brand. The typical goal of marketing is to generate interest in the product/services and create leads or prospects.

- On the other hand, sales activities are focused on converting prospects to actual paying customers. Selling involves directly interacting with the prospects to persuade them to purchase the product or service.

Marketing thus tends to focus on larger market segments or populations, whereas sales tends to focus on individuals or a small group of prospects.

So, for a large geographical region such as South-East Asia, a marketing plan may consider a number of the higher-level market segments which cross national boundaries, whereas the sales strategy will focus more closely on key individuals within a country.

Do we need a marketing/sales strategy?

Strategic plans cover not only 'where we are now?' and 'where do we want to be?', but also the methods of getting there. It is essential to formalize the answers to the questions into a plan that communicates the objectives and strategy to the management team to increase the chances of success. Without any plan or strategy it is highly likely that the organization will miss opportunities.

By following a structured process of preparing a marketing/sales strategy, and also of reviewing it from time to time (some organizations do this annually), organizations can help avoid major mistakes, and keep alert to changes in the market.

There are two very common and widespread analysis matrix tools often used in the planning process, both of which can help protect against major mistakes. These are well known by the acronyms SWOT and PESTLE. A main reason companies use both SWOT and PESTLE is because these tools offer broad and effective analyses of key areas of a strategic plan. SWOT is an acronym that stands for Strengths, Weaknesses, Opportunities and Threats. PESTLE has wider coverage of business and external issues, including Political, Economic, Social, Technological, Legal and Environmental factors. It is suggested that each of these tools be employed for each country under consideration as well as for a broader overview where a central operation is involved.

PESTLE and SWOT analyses

These are tools used to find out the current status and position of an organization in relation to their external environment. They can then be used as a basis for future planning and strategic management.

PESTLE analysis

The PESTLE analysis (sometimes referred to as PEST analysis) should be used to provide a context for the organization's role in relation to the external environment. It covers political, economic, social, technological, legal and environmental factors. It gives a bird's-eye view of the whole environment from the many different angles that one wants to check and keep a track of while focusing on a specific idea or plan.

The framework has undergone certain alterations over the years with some adding certain elements such as E for Ethics to be factored into the demographics while utilizing the framework to research the market.

There are certain questions that need to be asked when conducting this analysis, which give an idea of the underlying factors to be kept in mind. They are:

- What is the political situation of the country and how can it affect the industry?
- What are the prevalent economic factors?
- How much importance does culture have in the market and what are its determinants?
- What technological innovations are likely to pop up and affect the market structure?
- Is there any current legislation that regulates the industry or can there be any changes in the legislation for the industry?
- What are the environmental concerns for the industry?

It is critical to understand the complete depth of each letter of the PESTLE acronym, illustrated in Figure 4.4.1, if the process is to avoid leaving any gaps in the analysis.

FIGURE 4.4.1   The PESTLE process

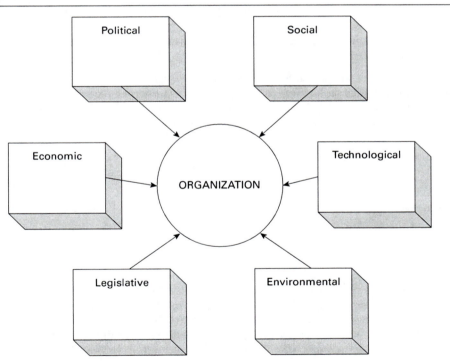

Gaps in the analysis may, of course, lead to unawareness of risks. The thorough PESTLE process consists of the following:

- **Political**: What are the key political drivers of relevance?
  - worldwide, national and government directives, funding council policies, national and local organizations' requirements, institutional policy.
- **Economic**: What are the important economic factors?
  - funding mechanisms and streams, business and enterprise directives, internal funding models, budgetary restrictions, income generation targets.
- **Social**: What are the main societal and cultural aspects?
  - social attitudes to education, particularly in relation to government directives and employment opportunities;
  - general lifestyle changes, changes in populations, demographic distributions and the impact of different mixes of cultures.
- **Technological**: What are current technology imperatives, changes and innovations?
  - major current and emerging technologies of relevance for teaching, research or administration.
- **Legal**: What current and impending legislation is affecting the role?
  - national proposed and passed legislation.
- **Environmental**: What are the environmental considerations, locally and further afield?
  - local, national and international environmental impacts, outcomes of political and social factors.

In carrying out the analysis it is usual to find a lot of crossover – for example, policies under political factors leading to legal and environmental factors. Do not worry too much about getting the categorization of the information absolutely correct. The framework must be holistic, taking the context as a whole.

SWOT analysis

SWOT stands for:

- strengths;
- weaknesses;
- opportunities;
- threats.

The well-known SWOT analysis, illustrated in Figure 4.4.2, remains a useful technique for understanding your organization's strengths and weaknesses, and for identifying both the opportunities open to you and the threats the organization faces.

Strengths and weaknesses are internal to the company (think: reputation, patents, location, resources, team, skills). You can change them over time but not without some work. Opportunities and threats are external (think: suppliers, competitors, prices). They are out there in the market, happening whether you like it or not. You can't change them.

To achieve the most complete, objective results, a SWOT analysis is best conducted by a group of people with different perspectives and stakes in your organization.

FIGURE 4.4.2 The SWOT analysis process

Management, sales, customer service, risk managers and even customers can all contribute valid insight. Moreover, the SWOT analysis process is an opportunity to bring your team together and encourage their participation in and adherence to your company's resulting strategy.

A SWOT analysis is typically conducted using a four-square SWOT analysis template (see Figure 4.4.3), but you could also just make a list for each category. Use the method that makes it easiest for you to organize and understand the results.

FIGURE 4.4.3 The SWOT analysis template

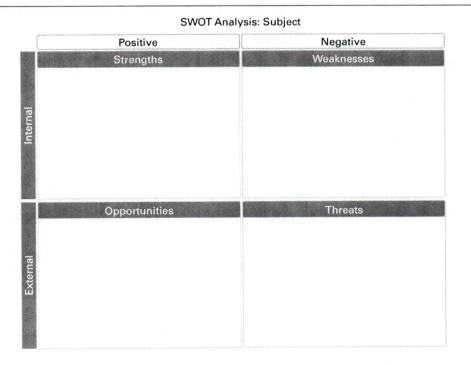

Typical questions to ask during a SWOT analysis are listed below.

Strengths (internal, positive factors) describe the positive attributes, tangible and intangible, internal to your organization:

- What do you do well?
- What internal resources do you have? Think about the following:
  - positive attributes of people, such as knowledge, background, education, credentials, network, reputation, or skills;
  - tangible assets of the company, such as capital, credit, existing customers or distribution channels, patents, or technology.
- What advantages do you have over your competition?
- Do you have strong research and development capabilities? Manufacturing facilities?
- What other positive aspects, internal to your business, add value or offer you a competitive advantage?

Weaknesses (internal, negative factors) are aspects of your business that detract from the value you offer or place you at a competitive disadvantage. You need to enhance these areas in order to compete with your best competitor:

- What factors that are within your control detract from your ability to obtain or maintain a competitive edge?
- What areas need improvement to accomplish your objectives or compete with your strongest competitor?
- What does your business lack (for example, expertise or access to skills or technology)?
- Does your business have limited resources?
- Is your business in a poor location?

Opportunities (external, positive factors) are external attractive factors that represent reasons your business is likely to prosper:

- What opportunities exist in your market or the environment that you can benefit from?
- Is the perception of your business positive?
- Has there been recent market growth or have there been other changes in the market that create an opportunity?
- Is the opportunity ongoing, or is there just a window for it? In other words, how critical is your timing?

Threats (external, negative factors) include external factors beyond your control that could place your strategy, or the business itself, at risk. You have no control over these, but you may benefit by having contingency plans to address them if they should occur:

- Who are your existing or potential competitors?
- What factors beyond your control could place your business at risk?

- Are there challenges created by an unfavourable trend or development that may lead to deteriorating revenues or profits?
- What situations might threaten your marketing efforts?
- Has there been a significant change in supplier prices or the availability of raw materials?
- What about shifts in consumer behaviour, the economy, or government regulations that could reduce your sales?
- Has a new product or technology been introduced that makes your products, equipment, or services obsolete?

Once you have identified and prioritized your SWOT results, you can use them to develop short-term and long-term strategies for your business. After all, the true value of this exercise is in using the results to maximize the positive influences on your business and minimize the negative ones.

The planning process

Companies typically go through strategic planning processes at least once per year. Doing so allows them to review the company's position and to reassess the strategic elements of SWOT and PESTLE. By conducting a reassessment, one can detect emerging strengths and opportunities as well as threats or external factors you need to address. Economic conditions fluctuate constantly. Social shifts and changes in values can affect the way the company's brand and products succeed in the market. Technology evolves quickly as well, so you need to consider opportunities for investment in technological advances.

As a rule, SWOT and PESTLE are first used during early stages of developing a business plan and strategy. SWOT allows you to consider strategic advantages that may help distinguish your business from competitors. Analysing weaknesses offers a reality check regarding possible concerns about potential customers. Opportunities and threats analysis helps determine the current and long-term viability of the business plan. With PESTLE, you also can consider the external factors that may positively or negatively affect the development of your business. For instance, some companies thrive during a tough economy, while many struggle because of more budget-conscious customers.

The final analysis

Using these tools as part of the planning process helps to identify risks (both internal and external) early in the planning process. Both tools appear deceptively simple but if used correctly are far more complex than they appear at first sight.

There is always the inherent risk of making incorrect assumptions when assessing these tools and even more fundamental, assuming that the information they contain is correct, accurate and up-to-date.

A final word of caution

When gathering information on markets in South-East Asia for use in a marketing/ sales strategy, one will quickly learn that the data are not so readily available as, for example, for Europe or the United States. Even seemingly reliable sources frequently contain patchy or out of date information gathered from incomplete data. So, when faced with the inevitable task of trying to analyse incomplete data, and to prepare a sales/marketing strategy based upon that analysis, there is a temptation is to 'fill in the blanks' with information that 'feels' right. But be prepared for a few surprises. The diverse markets in South-East Asia will throw up many surprises that simply do not conveniently conform to the planner's template. If there are gaps (and there will be) in the information required in the planning process, accept it, admit it, don't hide it. Don't add further risks to the ones that you already have.

Relative risk returns revisited

JONATHAN REUVID, HETHE MANAGEMENT SERVICES

Overview

The time has come to re-assess the relative risks of doing business in emerging markets, both collectively and individually, in comparison to those mature economies where economic recovery is taking hold. In the last edition of *Managing Business Risk,* we looked at Brazil, Russia, India, China (BRIC) and Thailand individually and South-East Asia as a whole. In the comparative analysis between these selected business environments, China and Brazil received the most favourable assessments with caveats about the political and regulatory backgrounds in both countries.

Even 18 months ago, the attractions of engagement with the BRIC countries were fading. Today observers with a penchant for puns would agree that the 'BRIC-work is crumbling' and in this concluding chapter of the 2014 edition we ask the question whether relative risk rewards from business with emerging economies in the short and medium term compare favourably with expansion in more developed markets.

The macro-evidence

As usual, the starting-point for the debate and evidence-based judgement is the current macro-economic data. Table 4.5.1 displays the latest GDP growth data for selected countries and regional groupings. Statistics for 2008 to 2011 (actual) are drawn from the OECD and those for 2012 (actual), 2013 (estimated), 2014 and 2015 (projections) from the International Monetary Fund (IMF) published data.

TABLE 4.5.1 Macro-economic comparatives: real GDP growth

% yoy growth	OECD Actual				IMF			
	2008	2009	2010	2011	2012 Actual	2013 Estimated	2014 Projected	2015 Projected
World output					3.1	3.0	3.7	3.9
Advanced economies					1.41	1.3	2.2	2.3
United States			2.5	1.8	2.8	1.9	2.9	3.0
Euro area					-0.7	-0.4	1.0	1.4
United Kingdom	-0.8	-5.2	1.7	1.1	0.3	1.7	2.4	2.2
Germany	1.1	-5.1	4.0	3.3	0.7	0.5	1.6	1.4
France	-0.1	-3.1	1.7	2.0	0.0	0.5	1.6	1.4
Japan	-1.0	-5.5	4.7	-0.6	1.4	1.7	1.7	1.0
Canada	0.7	-2.8	3.2	2.5	1.7	1.7	2.2	2.4
Other advanced economies					1.9	2.2	3.0	3.2
Emerging and developing economies					4.9	4.7	5.1	5.4
Brazil	5.2	-0.6	7.5	n/k	1.0	2.3	2.3	2.8
Russia	5.2	-7.8	4.5	4.3	3.4	1.5	2.0	2.5
India	4.9	9.1	10.4	n/k	3.2	4.4	5.4	6.4
China	9.6	9.2	10.4	9.5	7.7	7.7	7.5	7.3
South Africa	3.6	-1.5	3.1	3.5	2.5	1.8	2.8	3.3
Mexico	1.2	-6.0	5.3	3.9	3.7	1.2	3.0	3.5
Central and Eastern Europe					1.4	2/5	2/8	3.1
CIS (excluding Russia)					3.3	3.5	4.0	4.3
ASEAN-5					6.2	5.0	5.1	5.6
World growth based on market exchange rates					2.5	2.4	3.1	3.4
World trade volume (US $)					2.7	2.5	2.4	5.2
Consumer prices								
Advanced economies					2.0	1.4	1.7	1.8
Emerging and developing economies					6.0	6.1	5.6	5.3

SOURCE: OECD 15 November 2013/IMF January 2014

The upper half of the table records the performance of advanced economies: the euro area, specific country members of the G20 and a catch-all category of other advanced economies. The actual and estimated GDP data for the period 2008 through to 2013 show that all individual economies and the euro area were deeply scarred by the financial crisis and recession and that the euro area is not forecast to regain positive growth until this year. Looking through to 2015 the outlook for the United States, the UK and Canada is strongest. In Japan, France and Germany growth will be solid. More encouragingly, world output is forecast to continue growing robustly at above 3.0 per cent annually.

In the lower half of Table 4.5.1 the growth performance and projections for the BRIC countries together with South Africa are surveyed individually together with groupings for Central and Eastern Europe (CEE), the CIS (excluding Russia) and the ASEAN-5. Overall, growth for the emerging and developing economies is forecast to exceed 5.0 per cent through 2015 – three points higher than for the advanced economies – but this projection is weighted heavily by the individual forecasts for India and China. The Indian economy is expected to grow by 5.4 per cent in 2014, rising to 6.4 per cent in 2015. The glory days of annual growth above 9.0 per cent may be over for China, but the economy stills leads the pack with robust growth of 7.5 per cent for 2014 and 7.3 per cent for 2015.

The other individual economies were all hit in 2009 as the financial crisis reverberated across the world and have recovered in varying degrees. Brazil staged a strong recovery in 2009 but growth faltered in 2010 and 2011 and is not forecast to reach 2.8 per cent until 2015. In the expectation of weaker world oil and gas prices, the Russian economy is still growing at less than 2.0 per cent and is forecast to recover to 2.5 per cent in 2015 until the current Ukraine crisis. Mexico and South Africa look more robust with growth in excess of 3.0 per cent for each projected in 2015.

In third and fourth place behind China and India, the ASEAN-5 and CIS groupings present interesting challenges, with 2015 growth forecast at 5.6 and 4.3 per cent respectively. By definition, with the economic and political diversity of the individual countries, neither of these is a single market and market entry is correspondingly difficult.

As with world output, world growth based on market exchange rates is expected to exceed 3.0 per cent in 2014–2015. Confirming the positive global trends, world trade volume is forecast to reach 5.2 per cent in 2015. However, the statistics for consumer prices at the foot of Table 4.5.1 are perhaps less encouraging. Taken together, inflation in the advanced economies is rising gently and is forecast to remain below 2.0 per cent through 2015. Conversely, consumer prices in emerging and developing economies, taken together, was 6.1 per cent in 2013 and is expected to remain above 5.0 per cent. The implied good news is that goods manufactured in advanced economies are becoming more price competitive against the home-manufactured products of emerging and developing markets.

On the evidence of these macro-economic indicators, the emerging markets on which business people should concentrate their efforts in the medium and possibly long term are China and India, the two largest, while maintaining their focus on the United States, the UK and stronger EU partners, but there are other politico-economic considerations which need to be factored into this judgement. Before addressing these, let us step back into the global arena and recognize the socio-economic dilemma which the world faces and which will also impact our business decisions.

The socio-economic dilemma

In her delivery of the Richard Dimbleby Lecture in London on 3 February 2014, Christine Lagarde, Managing Director of the IMF took as her theme 'A new multi-lateralism for the 21st century'.[1] Reviewing the quantum leaps in technical innovation over the past century and the impact on global interactions since the end of World War II, she draws attention to the Bretton Woods meeting of 44 nations as the 'original multinational moment' and 'font of cooperation' which gave birth to the pillar institutions of the United Nations, the World Bank and the IMF. Thanks to the international cooperation that they have generated we are managing to recover from the recent global recession which could have plunged us into a Great Depression on the scale of the 1930s or worse. Looking ahead, Mme Lagarde identifies two broad currents that will likely dominate the coming decades: tensions in global inter-connections; and tensions in economic sustainability.

Tensions in global interconnections

On the one hand, the world is 'coming together' as a result of integration and modern interconnectivity where global supply chains service more than half manufactured imports and more than 70 per cent of total manufactured imports are intermediate goods or services. Typically today, a manufacturing company uses inputs from more than 35 different contractors worldwide. The communications revolution allows limitless information to be transmitted in the twinkling of an eye from limitless locations with the result that over the 20 years up to the 2008 crisis the share of international banking in global GDP grew by 250 per cent.

In consumer terms, Mme Lagarde notes that 3 million e-mails are sent every second between 3 billion people connected to each other on the internet with the highest rates of mobile penetration registered in Africa and Asia. The upside of stronger trade and financial connections is the potential released for tangible benefits through higher growth and a greater convergence of living standards, whereas the communications revolution can release creativity and spur change.

However, there is the potential for less comfortable outcomes:

- With trade and financial linkages on such a granular scale, minor tensions can be amplified and reverberate across the world with unpredictable results. Instability in the global economy can become magnified.
- High-speed interconnected communications can also be a two-edged sword. During 2013 we saw how the Arab Spring was both stimulated by Twitter messages and texts and also how the global platform can promote factionalism, intolerance and hatred.

This paradox is paralleled by the shift in global economic power from west to east and, to lesser degree, from north to south, which has been the defining mega trend of the past 30 years. Over the past 50 years the share of emerging markets and developing economies in global GDP has doubled from about one-quarter to one-half and is projected by Mme Lagarde to rise to as much as two-thirds over the next 10 years.

This shift in the tectonic plates of the world economy has been accompanied by complementary diffusions of power in the significant networks and institutions of which the fabric of global society is composed. The following are the predominant examples:

- Multinational corporations now control two-thirds of world trade. In terms of size, 12 are said to be represented among the top 100 economic bodies.
- 31 of the world's most powerful cities are also listed among the top 100 economic bodies. By 2030 about 60 per cent of the world's population is forecast to live in cities.
- By 2030, the global middle class could exceed 5 billion compared with 2 billion today. They will demand higher living standards and a greater role in society in terms of freedom, dignity and justice.
- The number of non-government organizations (NGOs) associated with the United Nations has risen from 700 to nearly 4,000 in the past 20 years.

In short, the challenge will be to manage the risks of a world that is more integrated economically and financially but more fragmented in terms of power, influence and decision-making.

Tensions in economic sustainability

The immediate priority for sustained growth recovery, as restated by Christine Lagarde, is to address the problems that are the legacy of recession: weak banking systems, high private and public debt, and structural impediments to competitiveness and growth. The three serious longer-term impediments to sustainable achievement are: demographic shifts; environmental degradation; and income inequality.

Demographic shifts

We have lived under the threat of overall global population growth and ageing, shrinking populations in developed markets, all of Europe and some major developing economies including China and India in the medium term. The realities are that in 2020, for the first time, there will be more people over 65 than children under 5, and that before 2050, there will be about 2 billion more inhabitants of Planet Earth of which three-quarters of a billion will be in the over-65 group. For the young countries, the challenge will be to generate sufficient jobs and the availability of quality education will be critical. Ageing countries face different, severe problems with the prospect of slowing growth at the same time as the social needs of a retiring generation will increase and need to be satisfied. China is sensitive to this challenge, but the recent change in policy from a mandatory one-child regime to two children will not avert the impact.

Environmental degradation

Environmental degradation is a newer and potentially more devastating challenge as more people with greater prosperity tax the natural environment to and beyond its limit. Within 20 years the issues arising from food, water and energy scarcity will affect us all. Already, much of Africa and the Indian sub-continent are afflicted with famine or malnutrition. (Conversely, the 2014 winter floods that the UK has experienced make a perverse mockery of the longer-term predicament that we all face.) Climate change is already wreaking havoc on the support that the most vulnerable have come to expect from nature. It has been suggested that by the 2030s some 40 per cent of the land used to grow maize in sub-Saharan Africa will no longer be able to bear that staple crop.

Whether the world will work together to phase out energy subsidies and tax energy properly – the obvious first step toward a solution – is doubtful. The World Trade Organization (WTO) remains becalmed and the prospect for concerted economic action in this direction seems remote. For now, we have to hope that participating countries will stick by their target Kyoto Protocol commitments to reduce greenhouse gas emissions. Encouragingly, Chapter 4.3 indicates that China is now actively engaged in addressing its environment issues.

Income inequality

Of the three long-term impediments to growth, income inequality is the one which individual government policies can address most effectively. Income inequality is rising in most countries and 7 out of 10 people worldwide now live in countries where inequality has risen in the past 30 years. The statistics are startling: according to Oxfam, 85 individuals have the same wealth as the bottom half of the world's population. The net worth of the Indian billionaire community has increased by 12 times in the last 15 years. Even in the United States, 95 per cent of all income gains since 2009 were captured by the richest 1 percent, while 90 per cent of the population became poorer. The same phenomenon is evident in the UK following the recession (see Table 4.5.2 later in this chapter).

Will multilateralism provide the solution?

In her dissertation Christine Lagarde pins her hopes for the future on effective multilateral cooperation through the medium of the United Nations (UN), the World Bank, the WTO and the IMF and the 'softer' instruments of the G20 and other nongovernmental organizations. The World Bank and the IMF have proven records of effectiveness, chiefly because, in the case of the former, it is a key source of funds for reconstruction and infrastructure projects and, in the case of the latter, the IMF is the lender of last resort for economies in difficulty. Membership makes sense, even for countries with permanently robust economies (if any still exist) because the health of every country's economy is interdependent on the health of others. The IMF has certainly confirmed its worth during the current crisis.

The UN and the WTO have more chequered histories. By reason of its composition, particularly that of the Security Council, political positions within the UN are so polarized that there is an in-built tendency for draft resolutions to end in deadlock. UN failure in achieving any resolution to the Israel–Palestine dispute over decades or healing the more recent divisions and insurrection in Syria are evidence of its impotence. Nor does the failure of the WTO to deliver progress on tariffs or trade restrictions since the Doha round in 2008 offer grounds for optimism.

The need for robust regulatory structures (a global financial system is probably still a pipedream) with global reach is self-evident. Financial oversight that is effective in curbing excess is clearly of paramount importance, but there are still countries where the will to banish corruption and elevate standards of corporate governance is weak or appears absent.

In summary, while Mme Lagarde's analysis of the socio-economic dilemma may be indisputable, the remedies which she outlines remain unconvincing. Therefore, in determining the regions and countries on which they should decide to focus their growth in the medium term, businesses should take into account the analysis together with the macro-economic comparatives and politico-economic outlooks as factors in making choices. There are strong arguments for avoiding those territories which are most vulnerable to the tensions described cogently in the Lagarde analysis.

Politico-economic considerations

There is one further macro-economic indicator which also has political connotations by reflecting the living standards and domestic spending power of local populations. In Table 4.5.2 I have summarized the OECD statistics for gross national income (GNI) per capita. The raw data has been converted into US dollars at purchasing power parity (PPP) to generate meaningful comparatives.

GNI per capita in the US is unrivalled at $52,547. Germany is the country nearest to the US with a GNI of £42,216 – well above the EU average of $33,673. The UK, France and Japan in descending order are also above EU average but tail Germany by 12.0 per cent in the case of the UK for whom the most sobering thought is that in 2012 domestic GNI was still marginally below its 2008 level.

For the emerging and developing economies available data does not extend beyond 2011 and for India not beyond 2008. The GNI per capita for Russia is relatively high at $21,701 (41.0 per cent of the US level) as a result of oil and gas revenue. However, while the Russian budget balanced at an oil price of $20 a barrel 10 years ago, a price of $103 is needed now and the price for Urals oil is currently $108.[2]

Nevertheless, Russian GNI certainly outstrips that of both China and India, while there is no data for Brazil. Although Chinese GNI progressed from $6,225 in 2008 to $8,334 in 2012 it still represented only 16.4 per cent of the US level, and in 2008 Indian GNI at $2,976 was less than 36.0 per cent of China's.

In assessing both consumer satisfaction and the relative attractions of doing business in China against India, we should also pay attention to comparative inflation and un-employment. China's consumer prices rose 2.6 per cent in 2013 with the Quarter 4 unemployment rate reported as 4.1 per cent. By contrast, in India consumer price inflation ran at 10.1 in 2013 and the last unemployment rate reported was 9.9 per cent for 2012.[3]

In a recent IMF working paper,[4] the estimated growth of different components between China, India and the South-East Asian economies is compared and analysed in terms of factors of productivity giving a relative measure for the dynamic of each economy. While the growth of human capital between China, India and the ASEAN-5 is similar, the growth rate of the potential labour force in China is currently less than

TABLE 4.5.2   Personal income comparatives: GNI per capita

US $ PPP	2008	2009	2010	2011	2012
Advanced economies					
United States	48,578	47,171	48,813	50,790	52,547
United Kingdom	37,355	35,208	36,029	36,574	37,333
European Union	31,967	31,047	31,790	32,571	33,675
Germany	37,547	36,528	38,463	40,627	42,216
France	34,769	34,418	35,106	36,261	36,672
Japan	34,622	32,505	34,413	34,890	36,306
Canada	38,493	37,212	38,397	n/k	n/k
Emerging and developing economies					
Russia	19,572	18,488	20,043	21,701	n/k
India	2,976	n/k	n/k	n/k	n/k
China	6,225	6,770	7,521	8,334	n/k
South Africa	10,065	9,987	10,322	10,725	n/k
Mexico	15,04	4,709	15,641	17,191	n/k

SOURCE: OECD 15 November 2013/IMF January 2014

0.5 per cent year-over-year against about 1.8 per cent for India. However, the growth of total factor productivity in China at more than 3.5 per cent year-over-year far outstrips that of India at around 2.0 per cent and all other countries in the region. Likewise the growth of China's physical capital has been consistently at around 11.0 per cent against that of India at just over 8.0 per cent.

In order to form opinions about the political stability and sustainability of each of the four largest developing economies, readers are referred to the preceding Chapters 4.2 by Carlo Gallo on Russia and 4.3 by James Pearson on China; and also in the previous edition of *Managing Business Risk* to Chapter 4.1 on Brazil by Geert Aalbers and Thomaz Favaro and Chapter 4.4 by Chietigj Bajpaee on India. There have been no significant changes in the overall risk assessments for either India or Brazil.

Both Russia and China are the beneficiaries of strong, centralized government. President Vladimir Putin's tsar-like grip on Russia shows no sign of slackening but the prospects for developing a competitive, broadly-based manufacturing industry in the foreseeable future remain dim. In China, by contrast, Mr Xi Jin Ping has consolidated his position rapidly as unchallenged leader since being appointed president and now dominates both China's political and business relationships with the outside world. There is no relaxation of the CCP's hold on domestic politics and economic policies but the government continues to support a positive transition from export and inward investment growth to a consumer-driven economy. The clampdown on corruption in the higher tiers of government and the abuses of corporate governance by directors are welcome signs of a determination to become a fully acceptable player in the wider international business community. Evidence of new-found engagement with the West is found in the British Government's commitment as Europe's central offshore hub to trade the renminbi in the City of London and China's significant investments in UK infrastructure.

On present performance, China also seems more likely to satisfy the IMF criteria for sustainability over the longer term than any of the other three BRIC countries.

The business decision

The conclusions of this review are fairly clear for British companies and entrepreneurs. For those with established business in North America or the recovering economies of the EU, there are sound prospects for continuing medium-term growth.

There remains a residual risk that the euro will founder and it would be wise to avoid or soft-pedal on development efforts in the stricken southern European markets for the time being. For those not already implanted in the US or the attractive EU markets, it is now safe to take the first steps. Market entry into the US is not easy and the frustrations of coming to terms with Brussels bureaucracy 'bound in by ink blots and rotten parchment bonds'[5] are daunting, but perseverance in both North America and in the stable parts of the EU is usually rewarded.

As for emerging and developing markets, only China stands up to scrutiny for early entry. China is already the world's second largest market and promises to overtake the US in terms of national GDP within the next 20 years. Throughout the past 20 years, since I have been writing about doing business in China, it has demanded attention; today the case for engagement is almost unanswerable.

The nature of preferred engagement may have shifted. Twenty years ago the most promising opportunities were for the formation of joint ventures in China to manufacture products at a more competitive factory cost, primarily for export and then for the domestic market. Today, with rising labour costs and increasing consumer purchasing power that logic is overturning. Manufacturers of consumer durables, eg the automotive original equipment manufacturers (OEMs), are now producing for the domestic market – the Chinese automotive market is already the biggest globally. For companies not already active in China, particularly those with prestige branded product, it may make better sense to build distribution networks in China as channels to market their goods manufactured outside China. Infrastructure in China, particularly in transport facilities is now growing rapidly, making effective national distribution a reality and removing one of the domestic barriers to trade for importers of consumer products. As always, choice of Chinese partner is critical but selection of quality partners has become easier as established entrepreneurial private companies and the commercially successful subsidiaries of state and local government with good track records multiply.

Therefore, one final word of advice. Develop your entry strategy fast and start quickly. Do not leave yourself out of the 21st century's biggest growth market.

Notes

1   http://www.imf.org/external/np/speeches/2014/020314.htm

2   *The Economist*, February 1st 2014

3   *The Economist*, February 1st 2014

4   *Potential Growth in Emerging Asia*, IMF Working Paper, 14 February 2014

5   William Shakespeare, *King Richard II*

APPENDIX

Contributors' contact list

Accenture Risk Management
1 Plantation Place
30 Fenchurch Street
London EC3M 3BD
Tel: +44 (0) 20 7844 4000
Contact: Laura Bishop
Tel: +44 (0) 20 7844 4650
E-mail: laura.n.bishop@accenture.com

BAE Systems Detica
110 Southwark Street
London SE1 0SU
Tel: +44 (0) 207 812 4000
Contact: Nick Wilding
E-mail: nick.wilding@baesystemsdetica.com

Baker & McKenzie LLP
Toronto
Brookfield Place
Bay/Wellington Tower
181 Bay Street, Suite 2100
Toronto, Ontario M5J 2T3
Canada
Tel: 001 (0) 416 865 6954
Contact: Theo Ling
E-mail: Theodore.Ling@bakermckenzie.com

London
100 New Bridge Street
London EC4V 6JA
Tel: +44 (0) 20 7919 1541
Contact: Ben Allgrove
E-mail: Ben.Allgrove@bakermckenzie.com

Burges Salmon LLP
One Glass Wharf
Bristol BS2 0ZX
Tel: +44 (0) 117 939 2000
Contact: Chris Jackson, Ian Tucker
E-mail: chris.jackson@burges.salmon.com; ian.tucker@burges.salmon.com

Dentons UKMEA LLP
One Fleet Place
London EC4M 7WS
Tel: +44 (0) 20 7246 7544
Contact: James Borshell
E-mail: james.borshell@dentons.com

Enquirisk
Rated Analysis (Enquirisk) Ltd
86-90 Paul Street, 3rd Floor
London EC2A 4NE
Tel: +44 (0) 79 6323 0069
Contact: Carlo Gallo
E-mail: contact@enquirisk.com

Allan Gifford
Tel: +44 (0) 7545 617 007
Contact: http://uk.linkedin.com/in/allangifford/

Stephen Gill Associates
Stanton Lodge
Aston on Trent
Derby DE72 2AH
Tel: +44 (0) 1332 793399
Contact: Stephen Gill
E-mail: steve@stephengill.associates.co.uk

A & L Goodbody
IFSC
North Wall Quay
Dublin
Eire
Tel: 00353 (0) 1 6492000
Contact: Sinead Kelly
E-mail: skelly@algoodbody.com

Hethe Management Services
Little Manor
Wroxton
Banbury
Oxfordshire OX15 6QE
Tel: +44 (0) 1295 738070
Contact: Jonathan Reuvid
E-mail: jreuvidembooks@aol.com

Institute of Risk Management
6 Lloyd's Avenue
London EC3N 3AX
Tel: +44 (0) 7709 9808
Contact: Steve Fowler
E-mail: steve.fowler@theirm.org

LRQA
LRQA Centre
Hiramford
Middlemarch Office Village
Siskin Drive
Coventry CV3 4JF
Tel: +44 (0) 24 7688 2386
Contact: Philippa Weare
E-mail: philippa.weare@lrqa.com

Gavin O'Toole
40 Grosvenor Avenue
Carshalton
Surrey SM5 3EW
Tel: +44 (0) 20 8296 9323
E-mail: gotoolewrite@gmail.com

Pacific Risk Advisors
20F Central Tower
28 Queen's Road, Central
Hong Kong
Tel: 00852 (0) 8199 0535
Contact: James Pearson
E-mail: james.pearson@pacificriskadvisors.com

Shepherd & Wedderburn LLP
1 Exchange Crescent
Conference Square
Edinburgh EH3 8UL
Tel: +44 (0) 131 473 5266
Contact: Katie Russell
E-mail: Katie.Russell@shepwedd.co.uk

Shoosmiths
Witan Gate House
500–600 Witan Gate West
Milton Keynes MK9 1SH
Tel: 03700 86 34000
Contact: Ron Reid
Tel: 03700 86 8471
International + 44(0) 1908 488471
E-mail: ron.reid@shoosmiths.co.uk

Squire Sanders LLP
7 Devonshire Square
London EC2M 4YH
Tel: +44 (0) 20 7655 1314
Contact: Henrietta Watchorn
E-mail: Henrietta.Watchorn@squiresanders.com

Stradley Ronon Stevens & Young LLP
2600 One Commerce Square
Philadelphia, PA 191103
USA
Tel: 001 215 564 8054
Contact: Bennett G Picker
E-mail: bpicker@stradley.com

XL Group
XL House
70 Gracechurch Street
London EC3V 0XL
Tel: +44 (0) 20 7933 7282
Contact: Paula Wilson
E-mail: paula.wilson@xlgroup.com

INDEX

NB: page numbers in *italic* indicate figures or tables

INDEX OF ADVERTISERS

CPSIA information can be obtained at www.ICGtesting.com
Printed in the USA
BVOW02*2230100714

358851BV00006B/10/P

9 780749 470432